The World of HORSES

The World of
HORSES
Judith Campbell

Hamlyn
London New York Sydney Toronto

Published by
THE HAMLYN PUBLISHING GROUP LIMITED
London · New York · Sydney · Toronto
Hamlyn House, Feltham, Middlesex, England
© Copyright 1969 The Hamlyn Publishing Group Limited
Reprinted 1971, 1972
Printed in Italy by Arnoldo Mondadori Editore, Verona
ISBN 0 600 03977 3

Contents

Royal horses

The Queen riding her famous
ex-racehorse, Agreement, now a
favourite with Princess Margaret

For centuries horses were an essential component of the regalia, of the majesty surrounding the throne. Darius, King of Persia, Alexander the Great, Saladin –that thorn in the side of the Crusaders – rulers like these were all brilliant horsemen. Their mastery of the magnificent animals they rode used to inspire and lead their followers into battle, and to the conquest of great empires. When monarchs ceased from the personal waging of war, fine horsemanship still added to their stature, and stables full of beautiful stallions and mares were a royal requisite. Even now teams of handsome carriage horses add a splendour to royal and state occasions that no motorcade, however resplendent, can ever equal.

The beautiful stabling at Buckingham Palace did not become the Royal Mews until 1825, a year after Nash–the eminent architect of the Royal Riding School built sixty years before–had re-designed the stables and coachhouses to their present elegance. Fashions in royal carriage horses change from time to time, and for many years the Royal Mews housed big Hanoverians, first imported by George I and kept then at Charing Cross. There were also the famed Creams, employed for all official occasions and bred at Hampton Court until the 1920s, when replacements became impossible to obtain because no fresh blood was available. For two years they were succeeded by black stallions, descendants of the Hanoverians, but since then the Mews have housed greys and bays.

Some of the bay horses come from Holland, strong, animals with good action and placid temperaments. They are Gelderlands, of the same excellent Dutch breed that draw the royal carriages when Queen Juliana drives in state through the streets of Amsterdam. Others are Cleveland Bays, versatile animals with their origins in the sturdy Yorkshire Chapman packhorses bred up with Thoroughbred blood. Modern Clevelands much resemble the elegant Yorkshire Coach Horses of Edwardian days. There is one Holstein horse; and a good-looking team of Oldenburgs, bought in 1967, made their first public appearance the following year, when they were driven to a park drag, one among the numbers of royal carriages paraded at the Royal Windsor Horse Show.

The famous Windsor Greys are not a specific breed but are well proportioned, eye-catching carriage horses, with the perfect manners and temperament vital for their work. One of the

Left
When foreign ambassadors are driven in state to present their credentials to the King at the Swedish Royal Palace, they travel in a royal coach drawn by four bay horses from the Royal Mews

Right
Princess Benedikte of Denmark is a keen and accomplished horse-woman. This photograph was taken in the grounds of Christianborg Castle in 1962.

Below
Prince Philip with his Akhal Teke
stallion, Melekush, a horse of such
excellent temperament that he is
now ridden in jumping and other
competitions by a lady rider

Right
Prince Bernhardt of the Nether-
lands is an ex-President of the
British Horse Society and a first-
class horseman. In 1954 he came
fifth in the Prix St George dressage
competition at the International
Horse Show.

present Greys is a half-bred Percheron, but originally they were small animals, almost ponies, kept at Windsor mainly for drawing the private carriages. Queen Victoria used four Windsor Greys harnessed to her beloved tartan-upholstered Balmoral Sociable, for most of her numerous expeditions. Moved to London in 1936, the Greys are now only ridden or taken by trailer to the Windsor Mews, for such brilliant occasions as Royal Ascot.

Grey horses seem to add to the splendours of ceremonial, their colour setting off the ornamented ancient trappings, the scarlet and gold Full State liveries of the coachmen and postillions. Eight Windsor Greys harnessed in pairs, the nearside horses postillion ridden, drew the superbly embellished Gold State Coach at the Queen's coronation, adding the final touch to a scene of unforgettable grandeur. The Coach has been used at every coronation since that of George IV, recorded in George III's reign as 'the new State Coach . . . the most superb and expensive of any ever built in this Kingdom.'

The Gold Coach may only proceed at the walk, unlike most of the other lovely vehicles that make up the royal collection. The Queen normally drives in the Irisn State Coach for the State Opening of Parliament, with Queen Alexandra's State Coach used for conveying the regalia on the same occasion. The Glass Coach is a favourite for royal weddings; a barouche often brings the Queen Mother to such events as the Trooping the Colour; there are Semi-State Landaus, Queen Victoria's favourite for ceremonies, when driven by postillions. These are often used for visiting Heads of State. The five Ascot Landaus are normally kept at Windsor Castle, for use in the Queen's procession up the Royal Ascot racecourse. All these elegant carriages can be driven at the trot. The carriage horses are regularly driven in London, and a Clarence conveying the Queen's official dispatch-boxes, or a State Landau or King Edward VII's Town Coach taking new Ambassadors to present their credentials at the Palace, can frequently be seen threading its way through the traffic.

The Viennese-built gold State Coach used at the coronation of His Imperial Majesty the Shah of Iran, and that of the Empress and little Crown Prince Reza, were drawn by teams of beautiful grey horses, specially imported from Hungary to replace the heavier grey and bay Holsteins previously used on State

occasions. White plumes, set in gem-studded crowns, decorated the headpieces of the horses' bridles, and their entire harness, which was made in England, was of peacock blue leather with gold-plated buckles and fittings.

Six grey horses of Lipizzaner origin parade through Addis Ababa drawing the Emperor Haile Selassie's coach on ceremonial occasions, with four chestnuts of the same type for that of the Crown Prince.

The Hovstallet, the horse building attached to the Swedish Royal Mews, was built in 1894 with accommodation for 100. Part of this stabling, like that at Buckingham Palace, has been adapted to house the royal cars; the remainder is inhabited by the twenty or so horses that provide colour and grace for royal and State ceremonies. They are bay horses, Swedish-bred and as adaptable as the Cleveland Bays they resemble – being used also as saddle horses by

Below
Princess Muna collects saddlery from different countries. Here Jussor is decked out in superb Western tack.

Right
King Hussein of Jordan is a lover of speed. He appreciates the paces of Cavalcade, a stallion that was raced before coming to the Royal Stud.

members of the Royal Family, and for the equerries and outriders attendant upon processions.

To settle an argument, in the year 1768 the Danish Master of Horse wagered the British Ambassador to the Copenhagen Court 1,000 golden ducats that Denmark's famous Frederiksborg horses, systematically bred since 1559, were of equal merit to the English 'Coursers'. The Ambassador could choose any one of the five Frederiksborgs in the Royal Mews; and after two weeks' training, and ridden by a stable boy, the horse had to cover in forty-five minutes the twenty-two miles between Copenhagen and that romantic castle from which the breed gets its name.

The day arrived, watches were synchronized, the King, the Court and most of the city turned out to watch this curious 'race'. Away went the gallant little leopard-spotted horse, and forty-two minutes later clattered over the drawbridge to Frederiksborg Castle – only to drop dead as he was led away to the stable. The body of this game champion of his breed may be seen today, preserved with honour in one of the Castle rooms.

Frederiksborgs still exist but, although retaining many of the original characteristics, they are now medium-heavy agricultural horses. For a whole century the royal stabling was filled with Danish-bred Oldenburgs, but this breed also became too heavy for carriage work after the last war. Now ten bright bay Holsteins provide two teams for State functions, and are housed within the lovely, stirrup-shaped department of the Royal Mews in Copenhagen – occupying stabling built originally for 250 horses.

The horses that live in the dazzling white, Spanish designed royal stables in Amman, have a different role in life from these other royal animals. They are the nucleus from which the true, pure-bred lines of desert Arabians are being preserved in Jordan. Today there are not many completely 'asil' (pure-bred) Arabian horses in this part of the Near East, and King Hussein determined to secure the fast-disappearing ancient bloodlines, that now make the horses of the Royal Jordanian Stud a valuable as well as beautiful asset to his country.

Princess Muna became very interested in this worthwhile project, and shared with the Royal Horsemaster and his

The Jordanian royal stallions are so well behaved that they are ridden in each other's company and with mares

wife in the exciting work of finding the initial few animals with which the stud was founded. There were one or two aged horses that once belonged to the King's grandfather, such as Farha, an old chestnut mare of a famous strain who eventually produced a hoped-for colt foal. The black stallion Negrito of revered ancestry, quiet under saddle but a demon to handle, arrived as a present to the King from a desert Sheikh. Gazella, sired by the great Seglawi Sherifi and almost priceless as a brood mare, was discovered by chance pulling a Bedouin plough. Shammah, also of a prized blood line, is an ex-police mare. And the classically beautiful Mehrez, discovered quite recently, possesses the valued and now rarely seen pinkish markings which are similar to those of Lord Oxford's famed Bloody Shouldered Arabian, brought to England about 1717.

All these lovely horses now constitute a famous breeding stud, the young stock being sold for very high prices around the world. Many of them, including the breeding stallions, are also used as saddle horses, combining the fiery beauty of their kind with excellent manners. Princess Muna's favourite, Jussor, a chestnut Kubeyshan stallion, blends the typical Arabian horse's high spirit and looks with intelligence and gentleness.

Rolf, the late King Christian X's favourite charger, was also a gentle-natured horse. In 1937, when riding through the rejoicing crowds cramming the streets of Copenhagen to celebrate his twenty-fifth jubilee, the King found himself completely hemmed in. Eventually the police cleared a way, but one over-enthusiastic lady, too stout to make the pace under her own steam, solved the problem by hanging on to the royal charger's tail. 'How lucky', remarked His Majesty later, 'that Rolf is so reliable!'

In the eighteenth century a Danish monarch and his courtiers often performed the knightly games of the formal carousel, for the delight of his subjects who filled the broad balconies of the magnificent indoor riding school. King Christian carried on the royal traditions of elegant horsemanship, and for thirty years rode one of his fine horses each morning through the streets of his capital city, unaccompanied except by the inevitable string of Copenhagen messenger-boys on their bicycles.

Even in 1912 this was an unusual habit for a monarch, but it proved effective on one occasion during 1920. One evening the King refused to sign a parliamentary bill, the country was in uproar and all military leave was cancelled. Then at 7.30 the next morning the Palace gates were opened and out rode the King, unescorted, business obviously as usual. The country heaved a sigh of relief. There was some rioting, the cabinet stood down and an election followed, but the King had remained unhustled.

On the fateful 9th April 1940, the Palace gates did open in vain. Overnight the Germans had attacked an unsuspecting Copenhagen and over-run the city. The Guards fought off an assault on Amelienborg Palace, but a truce was signed. That morning the gates swung open at the normal time to reveal the Guards, now steel-helmeted, presenting arms as usual. In the dark tunnel of the gateway was the King, sitting his big horse motionless, his eyes staring fixedly ahead. For a minute horse and rider remained unmoving, then the big gates swung slowly shut.

The Danish Queen Ingrid and the three Princesses are all keen riders, and about ten saddle horses are kept at the Royal Mews for their use, and for other members of the Royal Family and Court.

Queen Elizabeth II's riding horses are kept in the mews at Windsor Castle, and Her Majesty, a natural, sensitive horsewoman, rides whenever she can spare the time from her exacting life of public duty. Most horses go well for her, and two of the favourites at Windsor are the offspring of animals presented by Heads of State. Cossack was sired by the handsome little Russian Karabakh, Zaman, now on loan to a stud. Oporto is the well-mannered son of Bussaco, a fine Portuguese stallion which, like Zaman, the Queen much enjoyed as a hack before he too went to stud. Pride, a kind, gay little horse came from Jordan in 1958; both Belboy and Effingham were home bred at Sandringham; and Villefranche was one of the Queen Mother's steeplechasers.

Princess Margaret prefers Agreement, the Queen's once brilliant race-horse who counted the Doncaster Cup and the Goodwood Cup among his winnings before leg trouble turned him into a rather unco-operative royal hack.

Right
Kerima is perhaps the most beautiful mare ever bred at the Royal Jordanian Stud. Her profile is concave, her head small with a broad forehead tapering to the muzzle. Her eyes are large, ears delicately modelled, nostrils wide and thin edged, her throat set into the circular jowl with the distinctive arched curve of the breed.

Below
All Bedouin have a kinship with horses, and this royal Jordanian groom has taught Muftakher to say 'please'

Far right
King Hussein's daughter, Princess Alya, riding Shammah, a pure-bred mare which was found working as a police horse

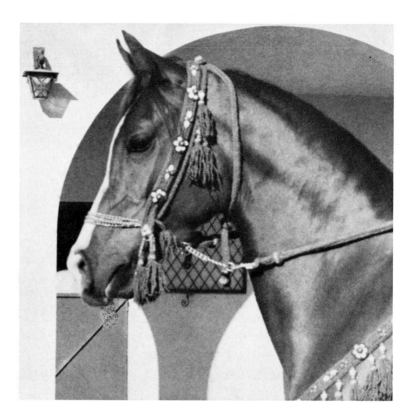

Melekush, a Russian Akhal Teke stallion, a metallic 'old gold' in colour, was given to Prince Philip by Mr. Khrushchev and Marshal Bulganin. He is now loaned to a lady rider, and is proving his wonderful temperament by competing successfully in riding club events and jumping shows.

Princess Anne has inherited the Queen's love of horses. Like Princess Benedikte, Denmark's 'Riding Princess', she is an excellent horsewoman, but whereas the King and Queen of Denmark's second daughter competes in show jumping and other competitions, Princess Anne does most of her competing in horse trials. She rides whenever she can, and despite little enough time for the sport, did well in several horse trials in 1968, riding a good young horse named Purple Star, loaned her by the Crown Equerry. Purple Star is an offspring of his ex-Olympic mare, Stella.

The Princess also enjoyed herself riding as a member of the Battle Riding Club team which, dressed in a picturesque uniform of days gone by, came second in the Quadrille competition staged at the 1968 Horse of the Year Show.

For many years Betsy, a black mare of much character but little blue blood, was the Queen's most constant companion during her rides in the perfect setting of Windsor Great Park, or galloping over the stubble fields surrounding Sandringham. Betsy is now retired to the home paddocks adjoining Hampton Court, the headquarters of the Royal Stud and home to about half the Queen's brood mares and young stock. Two stallions are housed at Sandringham, and the famous Aureole stands at the nearby Wolferton Stud.

The Queen's interest in racing is well known, but her knowledge and enthusiasm extend far beyond the race-track. In her few leisure moments, snatched between State and public duties and the shared pursuits of her family, the Queen, aided by a 'wonder-

ful eye for a horse' and a photographic memory, has studied the intricate subject of the blood lines and breeding of Thoroughbred horses to become one of the world's authorities.

In 1959 the President of Pakistan presented the Queen with a handsome Thoroughbred of impeccable ancestry called Sultan. A horse, now old but very similar in looks and breeding, was presented to the Shah of Iran by the President at much the same time. The animal was used for racing, but now stands among the twenty-four favourite stallions housed in one building at the Royal Stud at Farahabad outside Tehran.

There are nearly 100 horses in all, mares for breeding, young horses still being schooled, Turkoman racehorses, the carriage horses and a miscellany of others, including ponies. But these privileged stallions are those kept for the Shah and the Empress, for other members of the Royal Family, and for the Royal Master of Horse.

Among them are many different breeds. Saad, a Turkish Jaff (Arab-like horses also found in Iran) was presented by the late President of Turkey; Shabrang, a coal-black Darashouli came from the hot deserts of the south; the now aged Koheylon Arabian from Saudi Arabia, was sent as a five year old by King Saud. This is a flea-bitten grey which, like the Jordanian stallion Mehrez, shows the prized 'bloody shouldered' colouring, and which was ridden by the Shah for ten years, mouflon hunting among the crags and boulders of the Elburz range. There is a black Kurdish from the south-west, small but full of stamina, and the tough, locally bred Saar—the Starling—believed by the present Master of Horse to be one of the finest horses in the world for mountain riding. There is the dark bay Shabrow, a perfect example of the Turkoman breed, a horse of fine manners to match his looks, who is ridden by Her Imperial Majesty Farah Pahlavi, Empress of Iran. And there is the nucleus of magnificent animals trained specifically for the Shah's pleasure.

As the only monarch ever to stage his own 'revolution', an entire reconstitution of his country for the benefit of his people, the Shah has little enough leisure nowadays, even for the favourite sport of riding. But His Majesty remains one of those rare horsemen who seems to become part of his horse the moment he is in the saddle.

Tuned to the exhilaration of speed, and a lover of the freedom provided by the vast acreages of the royal hunting pre-

Left
His Imperial Majesty the Shah,
an exceptionally fine horseman,
riding Azar, his magnificent Anglo-
Persian ceremonial horse

Right
King Christian X of Denmark used
to ride every day through the streets
of Copenhagen. Here he is
presented with a bouquet of
flowers by one of his younger
subjects.

Below
The splendid stallion ridden by
King Hassan II of Morocco on his
way to the Mosque comes from the
Royal Stud at Tamara outside
Rabat

Below
Princess Anne and Purple Star are keen and successful competitors in horse trials

Right above
At the age of six His Royal Highness Reza Pahlavi, Crown Prince of Iran, rode a horse called Palang

Right below
The Royal Mews in Copenhagen houses ten bay Holsteins which provide two teams for Danish State functions. Ten riding horses are in their boxes on the other side behind the Royal Ring Master.

serves, the Shah requires horses that stand rock-like until with the lightest pressure they extend in a spectacular gallop. They must be horses of good stature, yet small enough to remain sure-footed on the rugged, precipitous mountain trails, and with the stamina for expeditions that can extend into many hours. They must be beautiful, and as spirited as the unbelievably fiery Khoshrow, a bay Bajalan Arab with looks to match his ardour. Some of the pleasure horses, like the good-

looking Anglo-Persian Tahmtahn, are sired by animals with Thoroughbred blood, a cross that adds height to the naturally tall Persian Arab. For hunting the Shah often favours another very fast Bajalan Arab, the grey Jadran, but there is one stallion, a chestnut half-brother to Tahmtahn, who is schooled to restrain his natural fire for the particular duty required of him. This is Azar, named for the Shah's chosen month, when the sun's fierce summer heat is tempered and the tall aspen

trees, sentinel around the Royal Model Farm at Khojeer, quiver in every shade of rusty red and gold. Azar, a magnificent creature with the superb crest and bearing proper to his role, is the Shah's ceremonial charger.

To see one or another of these royal stallions loosed in the paddock, is to watch the very perfection of grace and speed; yet once the lovely cavortings are done with there is no difficulty over catching—and Saar the Starling returns to his stable ridden bareback at the canter, controlled only by a lock of his silky mane.

Including the stallions, mares, brood mares and children's ponies, there are over 500 horses in the Imperial Stables at Addis Ababa. Ethiopian horses, like those the Queen enjoyed riding out with the Emperor on her visit to his country; Thoroughbreds of French, English and Australian descent; Roman-nosed Sudanese, known as Dongolas; Arabian horses, fine Hanoverians, and the Lipizzaner carriage horses.

All these breeds have their different uses. Some are hacked, some raced, some show-jumped or shown by the Crown Prince and his sons. There are those used for polo, and those kept for parades and ceremonial occasions.

His Majesty Haile Selassie is very fond of riding and does so whenever time permits. His favourite horses are housed near the Royal Palace, including Robespierre, a Thoroughbred now at stud who was presented by the Queen at the time of her visit. Like the Queen, the Emperor enjoys visiting his horses and goes to see them every evening he is free.

All these royal horses, whether at Farahabad or Copenhagen, at Amman, The Hague, or Addis Ababa, in the Swedish Royal Mews or at Windsor Castle, provide more than exercise and something of the prestige of bygone years. These beautiful horses supply the interest and relaxation vital for those who spend their lives in the glaring limelight of public duty.

ceremonial
&military
horses

The gallop past of the King's Troop, Royal Horse Artillery. The teams consist of six horses with three riders to each swaying gun carriage.

In winter the Life Guards keep warm in their long, red cloaks. The other regiment of Household Cavalry, the Royal Horse Guards, were nicknamed the Blues from the colour of their cloaks and tunics.

posse of horsemen clatter out of Wellington Barracks and cross Birdcage Walk. As they jingle between the Palace and the Queen Victoria Memorial, the troop give the Royal Salute, eyes left, and a trumpeter sounds a short Royal Trumpet Salute. They ride on up the centre of the Mall, sloping swords as they pass St James's Palace, and if the Adjutant has had a lengthy inspection that morning, may break into an unofficial trot before wheeling right to Horse Guards Parade.

These are Household Cavalry, men and horses of the Long Guard, which is reduced to the Short Guard without trumpeter or Squadron Standard when the Queen is out of London. With the exception of a grey for the trumpeter, the horses are always black; but on one morning the cavalrymen's uniform will be that of the Life Guards, with white plumes, red tunics or cloaks, and white sheepskins over their saddles. On the next it will be the scarlet plumes, black bearskin saddle covers, and the deep blue tunics or cloaks that long ago earned the Royal Horse Guards their nickname of the Blues. In March 1969 this regiment amalgamated with the Royal Dragoons, to become the Blues and Royals.

This Queen's Life Guard rides out each morning to mount the guard at 11 a.m. at Whitehall, and to provide sentries throughout the day until 4 p.m. A traditional relic from when the British ruler lived at Whitehall Palace, and later with St James's Park then closed to the public, Horse Guards Arch still provided the only access to the Sovereign's residence, which was St James's Palace from 1699–1762, and Buckingham Palace from 1762 onwards. Even when the new Trafalgar Square and the Mall formed an impressive approach to this Palace, Queen Victoria decreed that Horse Guards would remain the official entrance.

There are two unmounted sentries on guard at Whitehall, besides the two famous 'boxmen' (the mounted sentries) – the most coveted assignment, awarded each day to the best turned out men. Four horses do this daily duty, changing over every hour. They stand like statues, oblivious alike of the endless streams of traffic rumbling by, and of the admiring crowds of sight-seers.

Little perturbs the black horses of the Household Cavalry. Bought as three or four year olds, chiefly in Ireland, the most difficult training problem is to accustom each horse to the sword

scabbard hanging down its side. The majority of the horses continue working well into their teens. One revered mare, long past twenty, continues her tour of duty and is almost as sprightly as when she competed against such show-jumping giants as Pat Smythe's Tosca, and was considered for the Olympic team at Helsinki.

The Life Guards were formed from the Cavalier gentlemen who accompanied Charles II into exile and returned with him to London. The Blues originated as one of Cromwell's regiments of Heavy Horse, also incorporated into the standing army by Charles II. They became Household Cavalry in recognition of their fine service at Waterloo.

The Household Cavalry share in the whole Brigade of Guard's proud record on active service. Mechanized early in the last war, the cavalrymen serve in the mounted squadrons for a limited time before abandoning horses for armoured cars. Despite the exacting routine, the majority of the men enjoy their time with the horses, and have a fund of stories concerning their chargers.

A nervous, very new recruit was ordered to groom the first horse among

The famous drum horses of the Household Cavalry are always either piebald (black and white) or skewbald (brown and white). They must have perfect manners and be big and strong enough to support the great weight of the drums.

the twenty-four standing in equal lines each side of a central gangway. Alone but for the horses, he put his grooming implements on the manger and went to fetch a bucket. On his return they had vanished. He searched unavailingly while terrible charges, 'Misappropriation of brushes, horses, for the use of ..' filled his mind. Then the young recruit noticed that twelve heads were turned to watch his every move with more than ordinary interest, and he had a brainwave. He located those brushes in the manger of the stall furthest from him ... and he learned two unforgettable lessons. Why it is an Army offence to leave grooming implements on a manger –

and whatever anyone says to the contrary, horses do have a sense of humour.

The Household Cavalry drum horses are some of the best known, best trained animals in the world. They are always eye-catching piebalds or skewbalds, docile, impressively large and strong to support the immense weight of the two solid silver drums. The drummers steer by reins attached to the stirrup irons, leaving their hands free, and when halted the drummer taps his horse behind its elbows with his toes so that it stretches into the stance of a show hackney.

Hercules, the young drum horse to the Blues, understudy to their famous Hannibal, accompanied the detachment of Household Cavalry that performed the

magnificent tattoo, The Queen's Guards, throughout the United States in the autumn of 1968. His conduct was admirable and a credit to his original training, unusual for a drum horse, that included loose and ridden jumping, schooling at the canter, and dressage.

Military horses ceased to be operational in modern armies with the Second World War. But draught horses and cavalry were indispensable in the 1914-1918 war, and suffered terrible casualties. Quicksilver, a Royal Scot's Grey's charger, served three years in France, Belgium and Germany. Badly wounded by shrapnel at the Somme, he was unique in being awarded a wound stripe, the Mons Star, the War Ribbons of the Expeditionary Force, and the General Service and Victory Ribbons.

After the war Quicksilver joined the Metropolitan Mounted Police with his officer owner, who was appointed Assistant Commissioner and who for many years was a familiar sight in London as 'the man on the white horse.'

No motorized vehicles can add the impressive dignity to public spectacles of uniformed riders on well trained horses, and much of Britain's traditional ceremony is enriched by squadrons of the Household Cavalry. They have the honour of providing the Sovereign's Escort on such occasions as the State

Strenuous exercise for the Royal Jordanian Guard tent pegging with excitable little country-breds that know how to buck as well as gallop

Opening of Parliament, a royal wedding, or reception to a visiting Head of State. This is a prerogative of ceremonial duties shared by the cavalry of those countries that still retain them.

Le Guarde Royale are the corps d'élite of the Moroccan Army. They are also the King's personal troops, their duty to guard and tend him on State occasions at the Palace at Rabat, and when their ruler attends the Mosque on each Friday. The King, wearing plain white robes, rides to this religious ceremony on one of his superb stallions surroun-ded by Court dignitaries on foot, with a green velvet umbrella held over his head and detachments of Le Guarde Royale riding before and behind. The Guarde's fine stallions, twenty-five identically coloured animals to each platoon, are stabled at the splendid royal stud at Tamara, where their condition equals their surroundings.

The bodyguard to His Majesty Haile Selassie, Emperor of Ethiopia, escort him at all ceremonial parades. They ride Australian Walers—admirable and versatile horses descended from the famous Cape horses of Dutch, Spanish, Arab and Barb blood—which gained renown as remounts for the Indian Army and in the First World War.

In the autumn of 1967 when His Imperial Majesty Mohammed Pahlavi, Shahanshah of Iran, drove in splendour along the boulevards of Tehran to his coronation in the Golestan Palace, his magnificent entourage was attended by a Sovereign's Escort, mounted squadrons of the Imperial Guard, riding in advance and to the rear of the royal carriages. The officers bore naked swords, the troops with their blue cuirasses and scarlet-plumed helmets carried lances with blue pennants. Their horses, in matching troops of bay or chestnut, were decked out in full ceremonial trappings, including blue and gold saddle cloths, and immaculate white leg spats. The Officer Commanding the Imperial Guard gained his Golden Spurs in the celebrated Cadre Noir of the French School of Equitation at Saumur. Innately excitable and impetuous, Persian horses are notoriously difficult to train for jumping, but the flowing French style of riding suits them well. They are first jumped loose in a circular manège, and at a later stage are impressive to watch as they are ridden over a formidable show jumping course at the Guards' mounted section barracks newly built near Farahabad. When the troops demonstrate trick riding in the enormous area of their parade ground, their horsemanship is breathtaking.

They come singly, riding diagonally with the deep blue sky above and the

snow capped mountains behind them.
First the Standard Bearer, the Regimental Colours standing out stiffly in the
breeze of his swift approach; then men
vaulting from side to side of their galloping horses, one with a sword between his teeth and his horse bridleless; men stand, a foot each on a horse,
straddling one or even two in the middle,
and as a climax an intrepid acrobat
turns over and over a short pole, hand-
held on the saddle bows of two speed-
ing horsemen.

This would be a striking display performed at the canter on stolid chargers;
executed at a flat out gallop with horses
as fiery as any in the world, it is a first-
class exhibition of what is called in
Farsi: 'horsemen-well-doing-it', mean-
ing 'good riding'.

Most cavalry units go in for sport and
displays. The Household Cavalry
mount a spectacular musical ride at the
annual Royal Tournament, and compete in show jumping, dressage competitions and eventing. Horses and men
get the opportunity to hunt with both
foxhounds and draghounds; and a
Household Cavalry charger thrives on
coming off sentry duty in the morning
and, after a feed and a rest, being boxed
off for a few hours out with hounds.

The Gardehusarregimentet, the Royal
Danish Hussars, mount musical rides
and admirable displays at shows and
expositions throughout Denmark during the summer. Founded as fast moving, hard hitting light cavalry by King
Frederik V in 1762, the regiment began
mechanizing long ago, but retained
two mounted units in service until after
the start of the Second World War. Re-
formed after the war as a fully armoured
regiment, one horse squadron remains

for ceremonial duties, such as Sovereign's Escort to King Frederik IX, and to
provide a mounted Honour Guard for
new ambassadors driving to present
their credentials to the King.

Officers and troopers volunteer for the
four months' training with the fifty Hussar horses, before returning to the
armoured units. Originally drawn from
the farming community, today's volun-
teers come from all walks of life, mostly
unconnected with horses; yet they take
great pride in learning horsemanship
and in keeping alive the regimental
traditions and motto: *In actis esto
volucris* – Be fast in action.

When cavalry was fully operational,
men's lives depended on having good
horses, and many of the Hussars' were
of Irish descent. The Germans took
these during the last war, but when the
Danish occupation ended in 1945 numbers of German horses remained, plus
a few of the original Hussar horses.
These last were survivors from German
Army service on the eastern front, discovered back in their own regimental
stalls. Today the quality Hussar horses
are mostly of the new 'Danish Sports
Horse' type, usually of German Hanoverian or Trakehner descent crossed
with Thoroughbreds, with Holstein for a
heavier cross. A few prized animals still
trace back to Irish mares.

The brilliant uniform of the Royal Hussars, blue and red and white, was de-
liberately chosen to strike terror into
enemy hearts during the charge. Their
capes, worn over the left shoulder, were
protection against sabre cuts, as were
the ornamental fringes and buttons.
The horses' State Kit bridles are dis-
tinctively decorated with shells that
came originally from the Indian Ocean.

Shells of this type have been used for
centuries as currency and ornament in
far-away areas of Asia and Africa.

On ceremonial occasions in Amman,
King Hussein's Royal Guard carry
lances with pennants in green, white,
and red with a white star, the colours of
the royal flag of Jordan. Similar lances
are frequently put to more energetic
use, when the Guards gallop full tilt,
often in pairs operating as one, to give a
display of tent-pegging, a sport at
which they excel. Until the 1967 Arab-
Israeli war, the unit sent tent-pegging
and show jumping teams to compete
with neighbouring Arab countries.

The Royal Guard are not part of the
Army but a detachment of the Jordanian Police Force, and some of their officers have attended courses at the
Metropolitan Mounted Police training
establishment at Imber Court which is
run much on Army lines. This accounts
for the unit's routine having a distinctly
British Army flavour. As with the
Household Cavalry, the Royal Guard
horses, all sturdy little country-breds of
Arabian blood, are tethered in long
stables of meticulous cleanliness. The
hours for 'stables', feeding and exercise tally with those of the British Army;
and for ordinary use the horses wear
British Army saddles and the ubiquitous Universal bit. When the horses are
marched off, two to a man, under the
command of an Orderly Sergeant for a
watering parade, were it not for the
sandy ground and the blazing sun one
might be back at Wellington Barracks.

Scattered around the world these fine
squadrons of cavalry remain, not just as
colourful relics of past glories but as an
essential reminder that man cannot
live by machines alone.

Arkle, jumping to the front where he always liked to be.

RACING
&RACEHORSES

To the racing fraternity of south-east England, Cauliflower does not necessarily mean a vegetable. To many the name signifies an elegant chestnut mare who, before her retirement, became almost a legend on the point-to-point and hunter-chase courses in Kent and neighbouring counties.

Cauliflower is by Colonist II, a doughty and popular old warrior who raced auspiciously for Sir Winston Churchill, long before the Queen bought the stallion and sent him to stud at Sandringham.

The mare inherited her sire's stamina and courage, but was so impossibly temperamental as a four-year-old that she was given away. A character of strong likes and dislikes, and equally strong reactions, Cauliflower found Tommy Southern's small yard and few loose boxes as much to her liking as she found their owner. She settled at once, showed none of her former peccadillos, and Tommy took his new acquisition hunting.

He kept well back out of the limelight until the field, hung up by an awkward big fence, jokingly suggested Tommy should give them a lead. A lead? With a difficult filly that had never seen hounds before? But eventually he called for room, and cantered her round into the fence. Cauliflower knew little of jump-

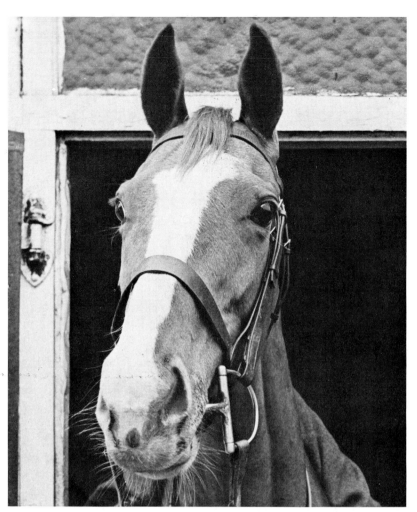

ing and nothing of hunting, but she cocked her ears, took hold of her bit and flew the fence – just as she did every fence she was to meet afterwards in her racing career.

Tommy Southern has a way with a horse. He learned to ride on the vanners of his youth, but was too busy earning a living to do anything more about a love of horses until after the last war. Then he bought two Thoroughbreds for £50 apiece at Newmarket Sales, and rode one of them in a point-to-point soon afterwards.

Neither jockey nor horse had been on a racecourse before, but Tommy sat tight, the horse 'went like the clappers' the whole way round, and to their mutual surprise, they won.

Now Tommy Southern has forgotten how many races he has ridden, how many he has won. He still hunts, schools over fences, rises at 4 a.m. to exercise his horses before work, and does them again in the evening. Not long before he gave up racing, on his way to the start, Tommy overheard a lady punter exclaim: 'So that's the favourite I've bet on ... well, I wouldn't have if I'd known it was being ridden by a grey-haired old so-and-so like that!'

Tommy has owned and raced good animals like Celtic Cross whom he ran in the National, and little Sandpiper

with whom he won fourteen point-to-points. But none of them have occupied the same place in his heart as Cauliflower, even though he never rode her in a race himself.

Soon after she arrived, the mare contracted tetanus and should have died by all the rules. But Tommy propped her up with straw bales, massaged her emaciated frame for hours on end, and combined with Cauliflower's own indomitable courage to save her life. She knew what was required, and although eating was impossible she sucked up the juice from the grain and beans that Mrs. Southern boiled for her, and so slowly returned to life.

Maybe it was the care she was given then that made Cauliflower so attached to her own 'family' and home. She remains suspicious of strangers and appeared a hot handful racing, but in her stable or at exercise in even the heaviest traffic, there was never an easier, sweeter tempered horse.

Cauliflower won twenty-three races. She went to the Aldington Point-to-Point six years running and was never beaten, and to Wye racecourse to take the Hunter-Chase three years in a line. She retired to stud, slipped her foal, and came back into training to win her last three races. When Tommy brought her home after she and his son Peter

had triumphed in the Champion Hunterchase at Folkestone, he patted the thirteen-year-old mare's neck. 'That's it, old lady,' he told her. 'No worse horse is ever going to beat you – you're going to finish on top!' And now Cauliflower has a chestnut daughter, the dead spit of herself.

Not all racehorses can be successful, but that makes no difference to those who own or ride them for the love of it. It is the horses themselves that count.

A Sussex lady owner has kept horses in training ever since a racehorse was her bridegroom's gift, thirty years ago. She never bets, and her horses never win enough to cover their costs. But they provide her with wonderful days in the open air in good company, and with all the thrills, and dashed hopes, that spice race meetings for those who have a runner.

Generous Star was one of the most successful of her horses. A winner of ten races, he was also the unwitting cause of his owner's most embarrassing moment. A 'certainty' for a three-mile 'chase at Sandown, the horse slipped up at the first fence, ditched his jockey, and high-tailed off round the course with dangerously dangling

reins. His anxious owner, etiquette thrown to the winds, ducked under the rails and set off in pursuit, fur coat, handbag, binoculars and all. She successfully caught a horse – but unfortunately it was the wrong one.

Generous Star attended the start of the 1966 Derby. Not as a runner, but in the role of a beloved ex-racehorse, loaned to serve out his time in the splendidly kept ranks of the horses of the Metropolitan Mounted Police.

Despite mechanization there are still young Army officers whose ambition it is to win the Grand Military Cup. One such, with more keenness than cash, has managed to pick up several cheap animals with dubious veterinary and racing records. One underfed, over-raced grey stallion, given understanding and proper attention, proved most successful over hurdles and began to catch the public eye. Sadly it died before reaching its full potential, but taught its owner a deal about the art of racing. There were others as good, or better, and some that were plain bad. All added experience, but the one to which that young officer owes the most was his first. A grey point-to-pointer that jumped so big it catapulted its owner out of

The French horse Relko winning
the 1963 Derby. Many French
horses have come over the Channel
to take the Blue Ribbon of the Turf.

This swimming pool for horses at
Caulfield, Melbourne, ensures that
racehorses get sufficient exercise
without risking injury to their joints
on the hard training tracks during
the hot Australian summer

the saddle until he learned to give it sufficient rein, it ably demonstrated that some stayers, tailed off at the start, can yet produce a devastating burst of finishing speed, if the race is long enough.

Nowadays point-to-points are more sophisticated than they were some years before the Second World War when Pansy, of greater character than blood and with a furze-bush tail, trailed the field to the finishing post, while her owner stood in the stirrups to flourish a hunting crop at his cheering supporters. But these country meetings remain the cradle for many genuine novice horses – and riders – despite the money and professionalism that have arrived to stay.

The most famous race in the world dates back to 1780, when the 12th Earl of Derby tossed a coin with Sir Charles Bunbury – and won the right to give his name to this Blue Ribbon of the Turf.

All historic races possess a certain magic, but the very name 'Derby' produces a brand of its own. And part of the same enchantment surrounding Epsom Downs on Derby Day spreads to the Churchill Downs at Louisville, Kentucky, each first Saturday in May. It encompasses the best of American and other Thoroughbreds, at gentle exercise with their racing boys that morning, spreads later to the crowds, 100,000 strong, that keep the turnstiles

turning; grows through the hot day and mounting tension of the six previous races, until the climax when the stalls spring open and gleaming three-year-olds streak off around the watered track to contest the Kentucky Derby.

Far away in India the Calcutta Derby is worth £5,000; and in Africa the Kenya Derby, run over the Nairobi racetrack, takes place in January, when the cement-like conditions often favour locally bred horses more than the imported Thoroughbreds.

For years French horses have crossed the Channel to win many classic English races including the Derby, and French Thoroughbreds are of as high repute as the good prize money to be won on French racecourses. Yet although Louis XIV started the racing trend in France, subsequent political upheavals almost eclipsed high class horse breeding until Napoleon reorganized the French studs.

Race-day magic is very evident in Australia on the first Tuesday in November, when everyone contrives to listen in to the great racing and social event of the year. On the course at Flemington the Governor has an escort of smart mounted police; fashion models put on extravagant between-race parades; the elegantly turned out social élite arrive in Rolls-Royce cars with champagne and oyster lunches to

The horses come from all over Australia and New Zealand to compete for the celebrated Melbourne Cup, and the huge crowd dons its best clothes to support this big social event

Below
The field strung out around the
bend at a Wellington Racing Club
meeting in New Zealand

Right
Thoroughbred mares and foals at
Wattle Brae, one of the best horse-
breeding districts in Australia

Below right
The ladies have their own events
in Australian picnic races and
sometimes, as here, compete
against the men

sustain them, and excitement stirs the general masses to an almost tangible pitch of tension.

Down at the barrier the cream of the Australian and New Zealand Thoroughbreds line up. Live-wire embodiments of blue blood, of English origin, which with few exceptions have been bred for several generations on one or other of the splendid Australian or New Zealand studs. They're off! And in a little over three minutes the hot sun shines, as it has each year since 1861, on the sweat-streaked sinews of yet another winner of the celebrated Melbourne Cup.

Australians go racing any day they can, whether to the metropolitan and satellite city tracks, or out in the country where the runners may not be so high class but the fun is just as good. That goes for the picnic races, gay informal meetings where the ladies have their own events, and sometimes the day starts early with a pigeon shoot. 'Grass-feds only' have half the programme to themselves – and have to be on course some weeks before to ensure no one slips them a feed of corn. The tote is absent, there are more bars than bookies, and if the horses show little of grooming and sometimes less of looks, by the rules they must have raced before and be accustomed to starting barriers. They are sufficiently tough to run twice in one day.

When the racing, prize-giving and speeches are over, spectators, owners and jockeys alike gravitate to the barbecue pit, where they sit on their cars, washing down the steak with drink stashed away in the boot for that purpose, and stoking up ready for a night's dancing.

The winner of a picnic race gets little more than $A 50, but when the crowd at El Commandante roars 'se fuéron!' ('They're off!') the horses galloping on that Puerto Rican track may win from $4,000, to the $35,000 offered for a Classic.

Races are big social occasions for the lively Spanish-Americans of the Caribbean, the island courses excellently laid out and with as fine facilities as any in the world. The horses have not always matched up to the exceptional prize money, but now American animals have helped develop El Commandante's standards to their present height; the Barbadian native-bred runners at the Garrison Savannah racecourse are being rapidly improved; and British yearlings, imported for some time, now compete with local talent for the rich plums to be plucked at Jamaica's Caymanas Park.

Great race magic is not confined to flat racing. In 1837 a Liverpool innkeeper founded a 'chase that ten years later was called the Grand National Steeplechase, and was to become the greatest steeplechase in the world.

They say this form of racing began when a country squire urged his friends

to doff their muddy hunting coats in favour of nightshirts, before settling to an evening's drinking after the ardours of the chase. Hours later the moonlit steeple of a neighbouring village church caught the squire's by then befuddled eye, inspiring him to wager his friends a cask of rum he would beat them to it. Sleepy grooms saddled up the tired horses, and away they went hell-for-leather across country, with hedges and ditches forming up suddenly out of the shifting shadows, and the tails of the gentlemen's nightshirts fluttering in the breeze.

The Grand Pardubice has been run annually since 1874, when an Englishman went to Czechoslovakia to win it. He was the first of many British riders to participate in this internationally famous race of more than four miles, with thirty obstacles – including the formidable Thurn-Taxis, a five-and-a-half-foot high natural hedge, with sixteen feet of water lurking on the far side. Comparable in many ways to the Grand National, the Czechoslovakian race has one great difference to that at Aintree – in 1937 the winner was a woman, a remarkable horsewoman, the Countess Brandisová.

Although several Pardubice winners have come from the stud of dun horses founded by Count Kinsky for this particular race, many different breeds take part, including English Thoroughbreds. No doubt one or two of these hailed

Right
The Turkoman spectators also use
their horses as grandstands!

Far right
Taking corners at speed in a ski-
joring race at Kitzbuhel requires
skill and courage

Below right
Leaving the paddock at the Hialeah
Race Track, Florida

from Ireland, where they have been
breeding some of the world's best
steeplechasers for a long, long time.
The most famous Irish-bred of recent
years is Arkle–the small horse with the
heart of a lion, the leap of a stag and an
unprecedented fan mail, for whom the
handicappers had to alter the rules–to
give the other runners a chance!

'Chasers are not raced very young, but
in many countries Throughbreds are
raced on the flat as two-year-olds, and
have to learn a great deal as yearlings.
In England their education starts on the
lunge, wearing saddle and bit and
learning to obey verbal commands.

Time is vital, and there may be only two
or three days of this before the young
horses are backed. But maybe it helps
the lad in the saddle enduring a rough
ride, to know that the most difficult yearlings often make the best racehorses!

Stablemen experienced in breaking
these most valuable and temperamental of all horses are becoming rare, and
like the Americans more British trainers
now 'farm out' their yearlings to special-
ists. In the U.S.A. the majority of the
20,000 Thoroughbred foals estimated to
be born each year complete their initial
education in this way before going on to
the trainers.

In warm climates racehorses often do part of their fitness training swimming, three and a half minutes being equivalent to a six furlong gallop and considerably easier on the legs. At the Ocean Therapy Training Ranch near San Diego a semi-circular canal, filling each day with fresh seawater, is used for breaking as well as training. The horses are led from their corrals by ponymounted cowboys. The old hands plunge straight in, but hesitant youngsters are encouraged down the ramp by experienced handlers who face them, first walking backwards and then swimming back-stroke until confidence is gained. Each man then swims beside his horse, eventually backing it by mounting in the water and riding up the ramp.

Most horses enjoy water. Some expend a lot of energy in a short while, others swim for a relatively long time and need persuading to land. Many Australian trainers utilize the sea or tidal creeks. A Brisbane ferryman charges twenty cents (two shillings) to row a horse for a three minute swim, and others have specially constructed pools.

Australian racehorses are broken at eighteen months. Unlike the wild mobs of other days, the youngsters are not sold until they have been fully handled, bitted and lunged – but they are only given a maximum of a week to become accustomed to saddle and rider. Once broken, they have two to three months half-pace work before being spelled (rested), returning into training as two-year-olds in time for the October season. No Australian horse may race until it will line up quietly, and all two-year-olds have to pass official barrier trials, held by the State Turf Clubs just before October.

Top level racing is usually synonymous with Thoroughbreds, but the sport is no less exciting in countries where other breeds participate.

When the autumn race meeting takes place on the course outside Tehran, the snow is already creeping down the face of the Elburz mountains beyond; but the sun is still hot on the lengths of Persian carpet that lead from the royal helicopter landing ground to the dais where the Shah and his entourage sit. Flags flutter in a warm breeze, the sky is that intense blue that is the colour of Iran, and the lively crowd presses forward to take its pick of the runners.

There are horses with typical proud beauty and high-held plumed tails proclaiming their Arabian blood; speedy, silken-coated Darashouli from the State of Fars; and numerous, tough

Above
Arkle, ridden by Pat Taffe, after winning the Hennessey Gold Cup. This phenomenal little horse, thought by some to be the best of all steeplechasers, is now retired after a foot injury.

Right
The racecourse on Ascot Heath was laid out in 1711 by command of Queen Anne, and Royal Ascot is one of the events of the racing and social year. Honey Bear won the Queen's Vase in 1968.

country-breds, of mixed origins but inherently fiery natures, brought from every type of work to try their luck on the racecourse. Everywhere there are Turkoman horses, the breed that has been raced for centuries and makes the most successful Iranian racehorse. The Shah owns several splendid specimens, runners in some of the Tehran races, and even the young Crown Prince has his own Turkoman racehorse.

The majority of the Turkomans are brought by their owners by lorry, from their home south-east of the Caspian Sea. Most of the jockeys are young

Top
The Turkoman racer's rugs come
off for the track, then the seven
layers are replaced and the
stallion carries owner and jockey
back to the desert

Above
The Shah and the Empress enjoy
attending the races at Tehran

Right
American Thoroughbreds are
famous throughout the world.
This is one of the leading sires,
Buckpasser, with his groom Snowy.

boys, but there is one little old man with
a beard, reputed to be more than
seventy years old and father to thirty
children, who is the most renowned
jockey of them all.

The royal helicopter has swooped
out of the sky like a bird, and the royal
party have walked to their seats along
the carpeted path, then strewn with
flowers by small girls. A bell rings, the
crowd ceases its restless movement, a
punter dashes to the tote to buy one
more fifty rial unit, and the runners mill
around at the start, jockeying for position. Then a trumpet sounds and
Turkoman and Arab, Darashouli and
country-bred leap forward past the
elastic 'gate' for the beginning of a race
which varies between 1,800 and 3,000
metres, their hooves spurning sand and
dust to trail in a cloud behind them.

In many countries racing is big business, huge sums of money being won
and lost on the racecourse. But like the
Turkoman, who race chiefly for the
pride and love they have for their stallions, it is the horses that count with
those owners who fully appreciate the
Sport of Kings.

The Bedouin have always relied on
horses and camels. The suwwan,
the stony desert, has no effect on
the cushioned foot of a camel, and
these Bedouin horses are shod
right across the bottom of their
feet.

HORSES
OF THE
DESERT

Right
The Bedouin no longer raise horses as a livelihood, but they are still used for transport, racing and prestige

Far right
Turkoman are some of the finest horsemen in the world, and grow up with horses, learning to ride almost before they can walk

Below
A few Turkoman still keep herds of horses as they did before becoming prosperous farmers. The mares run semi-wild, the weaklings culled by the rigours of their environment, and come to drink each day when the water trough is filled.

The horse did not move, only at intervals turned its head as though to inspect probably the first woman, certainly the first European, ever to sit on its back. All round stretched the Turkoman 'Sahra', semi-desert pinkish coloured with some succulent, low-growing scrub. The sky was the colour of a green pearl, slashed to the west with the vivid orange and magenta fires of sunset, the grotesque silhouette of a string of camels bobbing their way across the brilliant backcloth.

Nearby, the Headman of the village made gestures at my husband as they stood in front of one of the beehive-shaped Turkoman homes. His hands were expressive: 'But why does the lady not move?'

My husband, preoccupied with keeping a wary eye on one of the village dogs, a crop-eared monster with crocodile teeth, gave me his attention long enough to make a 'get weaving!' grimace. Men in black lambswool hats, women showing trousers beneath their hand-embroidered robes, shy little girls, and small boys who looked an integral part of the bitless, saddleless horses they bestrode, all watched with an air of mystified solemnity. As for me, not for the first time I was regretting my foolish maxim — that to describe a horse adequately I must first ride it.

'Cho!' exclaimed the Headman suddenly — an explosive sound, midway between a sneeze and ejecting hot soup, which it seemed I should reproduce. The mimicry was poor, but my horse at once broke into a loping trot, the overall tension diminished, and my husband grinned his appreciation that we were at least under way.

We circled the cluster of dwellings, the increasingly rare circular 'tents' woven from reeds, with felt rooftops.

Left
The beautiful head of a desert
Arabian horse, Mehrez, a stallion
of the oldest blood lines, at the
Royal Jordanian Stud

Right
The Yemen is famed for its
intelligent horses, and Nsr, beloved
Yemeni stallion of Amadeo Guillot,
Italian Ambassador in Amman, has
brains to match his beauty. He and
his master bow to each other
before starting the business of the
day.

Below
Stable for a country-bred—a stone
stall unchanged in design from
those of centuries ago

More women came to the doorways, their fingers busy with bobbins of wool. Lop-eared sheep wandered between the tents, and chickens scattered from my path with squawks of outrage. Far ahead, where the desert humps into a series of clean cut sandhills, a bunch of mares appeared, galloping free and wild, their manes and tails flowing and their hooves throwing up clouds of dust.

My horse began to show a fixed resolve to join both the ladies and the Russian border not many kilometres beyond. If 'cho!' meant 'get going', what in heaven's name was the word for 'stop!'?

There was no great increase in speed, only an air of purpose about my horse that was alarming, especially since he ignored all known aids for turning or coming to a halt. Desperately I tried to recall a command recently employed with the Shahanshah's splendid stallions, far away at Farahabad on the other side of the Elburz range. And suddenly I had it . . . 'olà,' that magic equivalent to 'steady!', more French than Farsi and certainly not correct for a Turkoman horse, but maybe it was the soothing intonation, 'Oooooolà . . .', that did it. We turned, and walked decorously back to the village.

The Turkoman are said to be descended from remnants of the armies of Genghis Khan who remained to make their home in Russia. Some of the tribes have inhabited this corner of Iran, south-east of the Caspian Sea, for more than 300 years, a nomadic sheep, camel and traditionally horse-raising people, until the Shah's far-sighted policies for agricultural aid turned them into settled, prosperous farmers.

The Turkoman horses, greyhound built and bellyless like true desert horses, have a characteristic high head carriage and alert expression. They are an ancient breed, and the Akhal Teke, the finest strain and equally prized in Russia, are said to have been ridden by the 30,000 Bactrian horsemen who formed the Persian King Darius' cavalry. In Europe Akhal Tekes were known as Turkoman Atti. They were always chosen, because of their exceptional speed and endurance, to mount the bodyguard of the Caliphs of Baghdad.

Horses are no longer indispensable to the modern Turkoman, but there are always one or more in the offing. Some tribesmen still keep herds of mares running semi-wild. They fend for themselves, the strains improved by the law of the survival of the fittest, galloping once a day to the wells when the dust cloud from a jeep proclaims the arrival of someone to fill the water troughs. The much prized breeding stallions are hand-fed, tethered beside their masters' homes. A bridle attached to the surcingle keeps them more or less 'at attention' from the age of one, when they are first broken. The stallions are swathed in seven traditional layers of felt from head to tail, each covering having its name, and these insulate the horse against the summer's heat and the bitter cold of winter. The rugs remain on for riding, and are only removed for racing and for an evening's rubdown during the ten minute 'airing of the horse'. Pedigrees are not written,

but the Turkoman carry their horses' ancestry in their heads, back to seven or eight generations.

Once the harvest is garnered and the hot summer has cooled to the sparkling days of autumn, the tribal festivities begin. And whole families, many wearing their colourful traditional costume, converge on Gomgadghabous or wherever the races are being held. They come by jeep and lorry, on motor and pedal cycle and by cart. Hundreds ride in from the desert, sometimes two to a horse, looming through the clouds of blinding dust, astride their be-rugged, shoeless, fine-drawn stallions. They are urged on by the honks and tootings of the motorized traffic, and by the distant strains of a band sounding from the race-track.

Once there the sun shines through the dusty haze and a clearing breeze flutters the flags and garlands. Sometimes the Turkoman races are honoured by Royalty. They arrive by helicopter and are serenaded in the intervals by pretty young girls, dressed in exquisitely embroidered tribal robes or entertained by local horsemen performing feats of trick riding.

Smart soldiers keep the shifting crowds within bounds; and everywhere there are horses, some picketed by heel ropes, many acting as grandstands with two or three spectators per horse standing upright on their backs.

The jockeys ride around. They are all under fourteen years old and are usually the smallest and lightest member of the family, so that several are only aged about seven. Decked out in racing caps

and 'silks', their racing boots sometimes of the gumboot variety, they carry
short, flat Turkoman whips, and sit
their plaited-tailed stallions with a natural ease that owes nothing to the short-
stirrup crouching posture of more
conventional jockeys.

A soldier accompanies the big fields
down to the start. Some late comers
never make it, merely wheeling their
horses to gain an unofficial bonus of a
few hundred yards. It makes little difference. The races are long and are tests
of the exceptional stamina of the Turkoman horse, so that it all evens out in the
end. The last race may be eight miles
long, and some of the horses pounding
past the royal dais have shed their weary
young jockeys long before the final
circuits of the eliptical, sandy course.

Honour and prizes are heaped on the
winners, the sun begins to slip down
the intense blue sky, the royal helicopter takes off, and the horses, victorious
or not, each carry owner and jockey the
long miles back home into the desert.

Many people think that a breed related
to but even older than the Akhal Teke
was part ancestor of all Arabian horses,
and the Iranians claim that their tall,
straight-profiled Persian Arab horses
are an older breed by 2,000 years or
more than the smaller, more familiar
desert Arabians of the Near East. Whatever the truth, records bear out that the
Near Eastern variety were bred pure
(what the Bedouin call 'asil') and completely unsullied by any alien blood from
at least the seventh century. This was
feasible because the Bedouin are a nomadic people. They still live by grazing
flocks and herds, and have always been
confined by circumstances as well as by
wish to those tracts of desert that are
watered at irregular intervals by narrow
storms to produce the seasonal grazing
trails. They also rode, and were de-
pendent for life, on camels—desert
beasts, unable to live in well irrigated
areas, inhabiting arid lands that until
recently were impenetrable by any other
form of transport. This was why the Bedouin were able to keep to an almost
fanatical policy of inbreeding of a relatively small, much prized stock of
horses. Because by environment and by
intent the weaklings, the slow paced,
the unthrifty and less goodlooking were
culled for centuries, the most beautiful,
hardy, and in those days speedy race of
horses in the world was evolved.

Through the centuries trade and conquest spread these coveted Arabian
horses far beyond the regions of their
birth, but although they mated with
local mares, alien horses were not taken

There are still a few mounted
police patrols in Jordan. They find
their sure-footed, quick-moving
country-bred mares the best means
of getting to isolated villages or the
remote tents of the Bedouin.

back to the Arab countries. So it is that
the potent and valuable Arabian blood
has influenced practically every other
breed of horse in the world, including
Thoroughbreds, a relatively young
breed founded on three imported
Arabian sires, and now the fastest
racehorse on earth. But the Arabian
horse itself remained unsullied.

Many countries now possess magnificent studs of Arabian horses, but because environment and rich feeding
tend to change the type, some of these
animals are far removed from the original. The pure-bred desert Arabian is
small and wiry and finely chiselled. It
has large, lustrous eyes, slender pointed ears, the typical 'dished' concave
profile, a high-held plume of a tail, and
that indefinable proud 'look of eagles'
common to most horses bearing
Arabian blood. It is exceptionally intelligent, fiery yet docile, and possesses
outstanding stamina.

Today there are relatively few truly
'asil' horses left in the Near East.
Through the years many of the best
sires were sold abroad, and lately force
of circumstances has made the Bedouin less careful in the choice of stallions for their mares. Here and there a
stallion of the oldest blood lines still
graces the tents of a Sheikh far out in
the desert, or a mare of the purest lineage is located pulling a Bedouin plough.
But most of the horses nowadays, still
indispensable to the Bedouin way of
life, are sturdy country-breds of Arabian blood and character but lacking the
ancestry and beauty of those preserving
their race at the Royal Jordanian Stud.

There are an increasing number of
tractors and lorries in the desert, many
Sheikhs travel the world by car and jet
plane, and horse-breeding is no longer
a livelihood. But horses still have their
place, ploughing some pocket of plum-
coloured earth on a mountain side or
providing transport and prestige.

By and large Bedouin life has changed

little since the days of Abraham. It remains hard and simple, an endless
battle with an unyielding environment,
yet one no true tribesman would exchange. As darkness descends inside
the black hair tents, fierce Bedouin
faces may reflect the import of world
news relaid by a transistor radio, but the
hobbled camels still browse off scrub
and thorn outside. Black-faced sheep
with drooping horns, and ubiquitous
golden-eyed goats still huddle close to
the tents as they always have; and a
mare, ridden into camp that evening will
remain saddled and picketed like her
ancestors of old. The cocks still crow in
the tangy air of pre-dawn; goat kids with
woolly legs continue their age-old game
of leaping on and off the backs of still
recumbent sheep; new-born babies
wail, and a donkey cuts its rasping bray
in mid-note. There are still crumpled-
eared pi-dogs trotting by with a coveted
bone, goggle-eyed yearlings teasing
the tethered mare; chattering women
and children that grizzle. There is the
same scent of scrub-smoke and the
thick, greasy smell of warm wool as the
sheep stir, bleating and anxious for
their pasture. And as the bell-wether
jangles its whereabouts, the seeming
echo is provided by an old, old sound –
the ringing note of metal, as the aged
coffee maker pauses in the recurrent,
unchanging ritual of coffee making, to
strike his pestle on the rim of the mortar.

That bell-note remains the herald to a
new day even in this rocket age, and
despite the Bedouin's pride in a co-
operatively run tractor, the overnight
traveller emerging from the main tent
does not yet start up his car or jump
upon a motor-bike. He unhitches the
single coloured rope that serves as the
mare's reins, hoists himself into the
same type of padded saddle that the
Moors used when they invaded Spain,
and rides off over the flinty desert towards the sun, a huge orange orb rising
over the horizon.

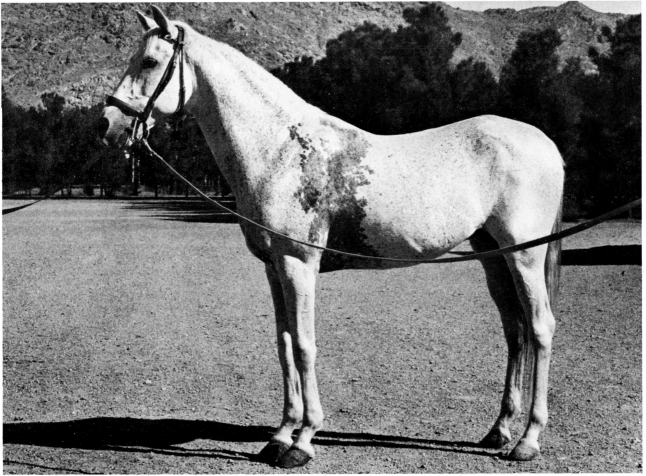

Working Horses

Previous page
The 'gardiens' of the Camargue
ride with the almost straight leg,
the Western style of all who spend
long working hours in the saddle

Above
Even in England tractors have not
entirely supplanted farm horses,
and the occasional pair still turns
up to contest a ploughing match

Right
Boatman Ted Smout and his
cartmare Rosie help to keep open
the old waterways of Britain with a
horse-drawn passenger barge
service on the Llangollen canal

Far right
The pattern of the cart used for
collecting milk churns in Wales has
altered little through the years,
but rubber tyres make it an easier
job for the horse

'TRACTORS, HORSES, PLOUGHS AND PLOUGHMEN ONLY'–the sign pointed to a field where ploughing matches and other rural festivities were taking place.

Up to the early 1930s 'TRACTORS' might have been the incongrous word on that notice, for there were still around 700,000 farm horses in England and Wales, until their sharp decline just before and after the Second World War. Then mechanization and shortage of horse-keeping labour almost routed them, and it seemed that soon the only heavy horses left in England would be the brewers' teams, and the few magnificent beasts bred for the show ring.

But that ploughing match took place in 1967. In the same year, the entry at one of the few remaining heavy horse shows was, most unexpectedly, larger than the previous year. Suddenly a few more farmers had discovered that a team of horses can be complementary to the tractors; that they can work heavy soil. under conditions where the machines must remain idle; that sometimes the smaller initial outlay and the lower running costs can make it good economy to add literal horse power to that of engines. They found that there are a few farm hands who still consider working with horses worth the chore of mucking out and feeding, on weekends as well as weekdays.

So, among others, there were teams of Shires at that ploughing match, noble descendants of the Great Horse of England, with huge, rounded rumps and 'feathered fetlocks', splendidly decked out in traditional finery of plumes and horse-brasses. And dotted around the countryside Suffolk Punches and Shires, Clydesdales and cross-breds are yet to be found, straining at traces attached to plough or harrow or dung-cart, their necks glistening with the sweat of their exertions– toiling in the service of man in much the same way as they have done since musketeers and cannon relegated heavy horses from the battlefield to the land.

Today there is at least one enterprising young couple who breed and break Shires and Suffolk Punches for a living; at least one estate owner who uses his home-bred Punches (a breed that is always chestnut and the only clean-legged heavy English draught horse) both on the farm and in the game-cart.

In times past much of Britain's heavy freight was transported by barges, 'long boats' drawn by horses, that glided along a network of canals. Now many of the canals are weed-choked, and most of the horses gone, but a cartmare called Rosie is helping to keep the Welsh waterways open. Her owner operates a horse-drawn passenger barge service on the Llangollen canal, and nowadays, as the result of a special contract, Rosie stamps along the towpath pulling a barge full of French tourists.

When the Lord Mayor drives in procession through the City of London, a coachman, one postillion riding the near-side leader, six grooms on foot, and two brakemen control the team of shire horses and the splendid, weighty coach

All horses enjoy going out to grass, and even these big brewer's Shires can frisk like overgrown foals

Surprisingly, statistics prove that the horses kept by some breweries earn more than prestige, and that on short hauls delivery by horse actually costs several shillings per barrel less than delivery by lorry. Whitbreads Brewery have kept a stable of Shire Horses in the City for many years, and twenty-eight huge, placid beasts still live there, working a full day on the City streets but with the well-earned privilege of an annual holiday at the Brewery's farm in Kent. Each year since 1954 six of these Shires, all greys, have been caparisoned in ancient, ornamental trappings and harnessed up to the four-and-a-half-ton, magnificent, gilt-encrusted Lord Mayor's Coach—to take their proud place in the traditional pageantry of the Lord Mayor's Show.

During the autumn, winter, and spring, when gales and fog make boat work chancy and shrimps appear close inshore, the Lancashire fishermen take to horses and carts to ply their trade. The horses are driven breast-high in the sea, pulling shallow-sided carts with the net trailed behind from a long beam. Occasionally there are anxious moments when a horse plunges deeper than intended and has to swim, with the cart, an involuntary Noah's Ark, floating along astern.

France has more breeds of heavy horse than any other country. Handsome Percherons, their quality linked to a kinship with Napoleon's Arabian stallions which he used as chargers; the Trait du Nord, particularly good in heavy going; massive Boulonnais, and the Ardennes—this last an ancient breed which is found in different forms all equally indispensable, in other lands including Austria and Belgium.

The Low Countries were known for centuries for their heavy horses, and in Belgium many are still worked on the farms. Small, cobby horses are used for draught in the local fish markets, and each summer on the last Sunday in June those at Ostend cease their toil for a while, to parade for the picturesque Blessing of the Sea.

Farm and draught horses are still at work in many Continental countries, but most of these are general-purpose animals. Man evolves animal breeds to suit his own needs, and the modern trend is for horses strong enough to cart and plough as required, but with sufficient quality for sports such as eventing and show jumping.

When the British first introduced skiing to Switzerland to found the Swiss winter sports industry, the alpine village transport was provided entirely by horse-drawn sleighs. Even today, with powerful cars gliding smoothly up and down the mountain roads, the sleigh driver with his decorative horses still plys for hire in the mountain resorts. His horses are usually large Swiss-bred animals of quality, with the occasional pair of Arabs to be seen in the more fashionable resorts. They are all decked out with plumes, or foxes' brushes hanging from their bridles, and the inevitable collar of bells that evoke the sound of Switzerland.

Sleigh horses are clipped but appear indifferent to the cold, standing for hours with only a rug over their loins, and maybe their numerous small feeds, eaten from nosebags, help to keep them warm. Thick, heavy shoes studded fore and aft give grip on the slippery slopes, and the horses keep to a rhythmic trot, up and down hill, covering an average twelve miles a day.

On the higher slopes where tractors are impracticable, smaller, more plebeian horses are used agriculturally, and still transport necessities in the more remote villages, hitched to primitive sledges by shafts connected directly to the collar.

In large villages all the work horses are stabled in a communal 'horse house'. In less sophisticated regions they still share quarters with the cows underneath their owners' homes, providing a form of mutual central heating. During the flower-filled Alpine summer, horses and men 'go up the mountain' to cart hay for winter forage, and to enjoy what a sleigh driver describes as 'a good time for us, and a good time for our horses'.

The numbers grow yearly less, but despite mechanization horses remain indispensable for some forms of work in almost every country. Cockney costers drive through the small hours with their willing little horses to collect vegetables from Covent Garden. And in the Isle of Man the Douglas trams are still horse-drawn during the tourist season—and prove profitable.

Today fleets of lorries thunder along the Iranian highways where once horse and camel caravans wended their slow way on the Silk Route; but for many years yet there will be a need for the quickstepping Persian horses, toting carts of merchandise through the outlying towns, or piled high with bales of cotton or sacks of rice in the Caspian littoral for the co-operative 'factories' where the crops are processed and milled. Similarly it is impossible to picture the streets of Gorgan or Gomgadghabous without Turkoman in high astrakhan hats, standing upright in

Mechanization has speeded up timber haulage, but heavy horses are still useful in the forest, here on the shores of Loch Awe, Argyllshire.

four-wheeled carts to drive their horses
at a spanking trot in and out of the traffic.

A few horse-drawn buggies, complete
with canopy and 'surrey-fringe', still
ply for tourist hire on the streets of
Hamilton in Bermuda. The horses in
Fiji are mostly descended from Australian animals, imported around the
beginning of this century to labour in
the sugar plantations. Many still work
there, but some are raced and numbers
are hired out for tourist riding. The
majority of these small horses are
'scrub' horses, but there are finer types,
spirited and of an uncertain temperament to match their speed – as one air-
line officer discovered when he tried
out a little stallion – and suffered a fast
take-off, an uncontrolled flight, and a
painful landing.

No machine yet equals the horse for
timber haulage deep in the forest.
Heavy horses are used for this work in
Britain, and the Finnish Draught toils in
the heart of northern forests. Modern
Russia does not possess anything
approaching the forty million horses of
the days before the Revolution, but still

Right
Rush hour street congestion in Tokyo is worse than in any other city, yet the Japanese police horses remain unperturbed and are indispensable for controlling the traffic

Below
During the summer Dutch mounted police patrol the sands of the Hague, ready to plunge in, horse and all, to rescue a child or throw a lifeline to a swimmer in difficulties

Far right
The Jamaican Mounted Police Troop was only formed in 1961. The ten hunter type horses perform all the usual duties of a police horse.

has need of them in that vast country. In the far north despite mechanization, there are still a few small, shaggy horses to cope with part of the 'izvoz' (transport over snow-covered trails) or lug the forest timber. Hard, primitive little beasts, undiluted by any soft alien blood, they have thick, coarse hair and layers of subcutaneous fat to withstand the daunting cold, and impenetrably tough skins to repel the hordes of biting summer insects.

In many countries horses continue to be employed to help keep the law, and like those of the remaining units of cavalry, police horses enhance state and ceremonial occasions. But even on such an unlikely venue as the congested streets and avenues of New York, some of that city's 270 mounted policemen help disentangle the traffic.

Traffic control, town and country patrol, promoting good relations with the public, these are the main duties of police horses working in cities as far apart as London and Tokyo, Sydney and Stuttgart, Birmingham and Boston and many more. Crowd control remains a job for which well trained horses are particularly suited, because their size and relative unfamiliarity still command respect and the mounted officer is high enough up to locate the source of any trouble.

The city of London horses and officers train, together with those from the other British towns and cities that retain a mounted force, at the Metropolitan Mounted Police training centre at Imber Court, in company also with officers from overseas forces. The horses' training takes an average of six to seven months, undertaken by officers chosen for their patience and firmness as well as their riding ability and experience. The schooling is based on the truth that relaxed, unfrightened horses are fully responsive to instruction. All types of 'nuisance training' renders the animals almost impervious to the strange sights, sounds and emotional impact of crowds. When training is completed, great care is taken to match the young horses with experienced officers to whom they are temperamentally suited.

Since 1948 the Metropolitan Mounted Police have had the honour of providing the Queen's horse at her official Birthday Parade, the Trooping the Colour, and these animals have become public characters.

Winston was the first, a horse of presence and military bearing with an obvious appreciation of ceremonial. He was succeeded by Imperial, another

The Tehran mounted police are armed with swords, and rifles which they fire from the saddle while their stallions stand rock still. They are provided with fibre-glass helmets for use in serious disturbances.

quality chestnut with exemplary parade manners, but who by temperament required all the Queen's tactful and understanding horsemanship. There are always two or three likely applicants for this honour, and for some years Neill, a big, brown horse, acted as first understudy. His chance came in 1967, when he behaved with dignity and perfect manners. The next year Neill and Doctor, the gentle grey that sometimes stood in for Imperial, were both lame and Fairway took over. This large, reliable, not over-goodlooking old horse carried the Duke of Gloucester for many years at the Trooping, becoming notable for his comfortable 'straddle' and the unobtrusive shuffle that nearly took him where he obviously wished to be—out of line with Prince Philip's mount and on station with the Queen's. In 1968, straddled at ease out in front of Horse Guard's Arch, accoutred in the beautiful State saddlery and the Queen's blue, gold-embroidered saddlecloth, Fairway contemplated the precise lines of Guardsmen marching before their Sovereign, the Household Cavalry jingling by, and never moved an inch. There was no need to, for he had finally 'made it.'

The Tehran Mounted Police ride

fiery stallions, unequalled for controlling boisterous Iranian crowds, or acting as powerful deterrents to the unlawful as they patrol the wide boulevards by night, padding along in the shadows cast by tall, aromatic-leaved plane trees.

The mounted division of the Barcelona Municipal Police, founded as a municipal guard in 1856, also ride stallions, fine Andalusian horses with a dual role in life. They perform the day to day duties normal to urban police horses—including a unique reverse advance with heels in evidence, most effective in controlling over-excited crowds—and also give public displays of dressage and a celebrated Carousel.

These colourful exhibitions of control and horsemanship are famous at many of the larger horse shows in Europe and Spain. The Carousel is also performed on Saturday and Wednesday nights throughout the summer as a tourist attraction in Barcelona. The illuminated performance, staged to music provided by the Police Band of Trumpeters, takes place in one of the parks, and is a triumph of equestrian schooling. The stallions exhibit beauty and obedience of the highest standard, at one point lining up to bow, a feat of

mission entirely foreign to the nature of an entire horse. As a finale the lights are extinguished, to come on again and illuminate the horses lying prone, each rider in his picturesque uniform standing upright on his stallion's shoulders.

The sixteen well schooled horses, mostly of Swedish or German antecedents, belonging to the mounted branch of the Copenhagen Police, have been used since 1882 for ceremonial, displays and patrol duties. They also do traffic control and have much the same responsibilities as the foot police. If needed the horses are called on as a 'persuasion remedy' for crowd control, but this duty is seldom necessary – either because the Copenhagen citizens are calm by nature, or because the mere factor of a mounted police unit acts as a deterrent.

The Dutch Mounted Police are trained to throw a lifeline to a swimmer in difficulties off The Hague, or to plunge in, the rider swimming beside his horse, to rescue a drowning child. The entire Lesotho police force is mounted, on tough little countrybreds ideal for patrols lasting days over trackless, mountainous terrain.

The few remaining horse patrols of the Jordanian police also ride country-breds – sure-footed little mares of Arabian blood, ideal for the rocky ground, and used for carrying messages or a summons to remote villages and the transient tents of the Bedouin.

Of all the world's police forces the 'Mounties', the Royal Canadian Mounted Police, have always caught the public's imagination. Proud descendants of the original North West Mounted Police who brought peace and justice to the vast Canadian territories, the Mounties are now fully mechanized. Their black horses are retained only for a few ceremonial occasions and to perform their famous musical ride whose complex manoeuvres have their roots in cavalry tradition.

Ever since man domesticated animals, shepherds and drovers have ridden to tend sheep, horses and cattle browsing the grazing trails or measureless expanses of prairie. The Mongolians, renowned horsemen through the centuries, add to their horse herds by galloping full tilt after a wild horse, and lassoing it with a loop on the end of a long pole.

The czikos, the Hungarian cowboys, ride to 'look' their huge herds of domestic animals just as they have always done, traversing the wide, dusty

Left
Even in New York there are still police horses working on traffic control

Right
The lovely horses and picturesque uniforms of the Carabinieri enhance the splendours of Rome

Below
The Queen Mother presented
Brig o' Dee to the Metropolitan
Mounted Police. He is an excellent
horse on street patrol and in traffic,
but will have nothing to do with
ceremonial.

Right
You can take a ride in a horse-
drawn tram at Douglas, Isle of Man

Hungarian plains – the pusztas – all through the long hot days of summer.

South and west of Hungary, the Golf du Lion laps a countryside where the mistral whines through the osiers, and crouching thorn and tangled olive are the landmarks of the mosquito-ridden, watery regions of the Camargue. Now the pink clouds of flamingos are vanishing in the face of tourists who are discovering this wild, fascinating corner of France. The landscape is changing before encroaching paddy fields of rice, but the black Camarguais bulls remain. These are bulls bred quick and light on the turn, and they do not suffer the *mise à mort* of their Spanish cousins, but live to battle again with twenty or so adversaries at a time, all trying to snatch the prized strings placed between the horns; bulls that can leap the barrera like a stag, that grow wiser and more militant with each fight, and that breed and live semi-wild, herded and worked by the 'gardiens' who ride the famous wild white horses of the sea.

Bred also for centuries in the same hard-living region, roaming free to forage for the rough grazing on which they survive, these small horses are exceptionally tough. Of an ancient lineage, their fine, long heads and sloping quarters show obvious Barb blood – that eastern breed whose origins like those of the Arabian are lost in time.

Until Hernan Cortes took fifteen horses with him to conquer Mexico, there had been no equines on the mainland of the New World since the first horse ancestors died out hundreds of thousands of years before. Cortes' horses were of Spanish and Portuguese breeding, many with the Arabian and Barb blood which were introduced into Spanish horses with the Moorish invasions. Large numbers escaped, to thrive and found the enormous feral herds of mustangs that spread eventually as far as the Canadian border.

In time these American mustangs lost some of the grace and size of their Spanish ancestors, but gained an exceptional stamina and intelligence. Many were caught and worked as old-time cow-ponies, and they are the foundation stock, bred up and improved, of the indispensable American Range horse of today.

The mustangs that spread south were the forebears of the South American Criollo, a versatile and enduring little horse, varying in type according to country and climate, but much nearer to the original than the North American horses. The Brazilian Crioulo, the Mangalargo of Sao Paulo, the Peruvian

Right
Mustering in the heat and
dust of tropical north Queensland

Below
Working cattle in
Australia's Northern Territory

Bottom
Gauchos are among the finest
rough riders in the world.
They work and live in small
groups, their horses as essential
to them as the air they breathe.

Right
The small, sometimes fiery horses of Fiji came originally from Australia. They work in plantations take tourists riding, and race.

Below
The Tehran Mounted Police find their spirited Persian stallions most effective for controlling crowds

Far right
Caravanning with a horse in Ireland makes a wonderful holiday. Skewbalds have always been associated with the gypsy way of life.

Costeño, the Venezuelan Llanero, these are all essentially much the same as the Criollo of the Argentine. They are all stocky, strong for their size, frugal feeders, of remarkable stamina, and are used as hard-working necessities in their particular countries. Many Criollos are range horses, still vital for tending the beef herds that form such an important part of South America's economy.

When those horses of long ago carried the frontiersmen to open up the North American continent, there were dangers in plenty—hostile Indians, wild animals, disease of man and beast, but there were rivers to provide water, game and pasture for food, and forests for shelter. When the first unwilling passengers of the convict hulks hoisted the Union Jack at Port Jackson in Australia, they found 'an unkept, uncanny and unknown' land. Great inhospitable expanses, where the plants, the animals, even the insects were totally alien, and the few inhabitants so primitive as to appear scarcely human. There were no horses in that apparently unfriendly land, but seven from the Cape of Good Hope were landed in 1799. English horse blood was introduced later to improve the quality, resulting within forty years in the Australian Waler, named from its State of origin, New South Wales.

A type more than a definite breed,

Walers provided the weight-carrying horses on which the old time Trooper Police relied to bring law, order and a welcome link with civilization to Australia's outback.

'The stock horse, ... ridden all day, turned out at night without cleaning or clothing, ... is shown the water, hobbled and left to care for himself ... in any season or any climate, ... and finds his only feed in the grass.... Day after day, for weeks of light work, or consecutive days of hard galloping after stock he continues this life ...'

Those words were written in 1873, and concerned Walers. They are equally applicable today, even though the modern stockhorse is more likely to be perhaps a Quarter Horse, occasionally an Arabian, or usually a Thoroughbred or Thoroughbred cross.

Despite more bituminized roads that make stock transport easy by road trains, it is still not uncommon for mobs of cattle to be walked thousands of miles across the continent. Cattle travel approximately eight miles a day, spread out over half a mile, and so long as the season is good they pick up condition as they go. For a drove that can take anything up to two years, most stockmen prefer the long, easy stride of a horse with Thoroughbred blood.

Droving nowadays is not quite the hazardous job it used to be. All the Government routes have water-bores

every fifteen miles or so, unlike the old
days when his own life and that of his
team and his cattle depended on the
drover knowing the thousands of miles
of country he crossed as well as the
back of his own hand.

It takes seven men to move 1,200 head
of cattle – the boss drover, four stockmen, a cook, and the horse tailer – who
helps the cook make night camp and is
responsible for the horses. He breaks
them and bells and hobbles some of
them at night for easy locating. In the
morning the horse tailer catches the
night horse, close hobbled to keep it
nearby, and rides (drives) the others
back to camp. But it sometimes happens that despite an all night watch
something, maybe a bird calling suddenly in the darkness, sets off the cattle
so that the whole mob rushes (stam-
pedes). Usually they stick together, and
as soon as it is light the stockmen try to
ring them, galloping up the wing and
turning the leaders, wheeling the racing
beasts through clouds of red dust and
endeavouring to mill or circle them back
to camp.

The drovers' lives are still largely cir-
cumscribed by the horses they ride.
And as light relief from the hours of

riding work, they compete in the ever popular rodeos. Events of buckjumping, bareback jumping, steer riding, bull-dogging, and calf roping, where the high prize money often tempts American rough riders to come over from the U.S.A. and do the rough riding circuit. Camp Drafts are another popular competition, peculiar to Australia, where a beast is cut out from a mob and taken around a specified course, the contest judged on time.

Despite an inherited horse lore that goes back less than two centuries, the Aborigines make fine horsemen, appreciative of good animals, and their kindness only failing occasionally through ignorance. They make first-class horse tailers and breakers, showing quick thinking in awkward situations, and love speed–sometimes allowing a beast to break away purposely so that they can gallop in chase. Some of the women make excellent stockwomen, and no one can better an Aborigine at tracking. They often ride bareback, mounting a horse by gripping its leg above the knee with a big toe, and then springing up.

For mustering, each property keeps roughly one horse for every eighty head of cattle. They used to reckon one horse for every 200 sheep, but the modern grazier often uses a motorbike which is more economical on the flatter country-side of his sheep station.

Properties are mustered as soon as 'the wet' has finished and, depending on size, the work can take up to four months. The men ride out on stock camps, mustering area by area, branding the calves, and driving the cattle to be sold back to the homestead for the drovers to take over. Cattle are more intelligent than sheep and can be hustled a little on these homeward treks, but sheep must go their own pace, otherwise they get flustered and run around in circles.

The majority of Australian properties possess dogs, often Kelpies, for helping with the stock. But the most prized stock dog is a blue speckled animal with a black or red face, and a tan spot over each eye. It is the only pure-bred cattle dog in the world, evolved from a mixture of Kelpie, Dalmation, Collie and wild Dingo, registered in 1890, with a hardiness matched by the intelligence it has developed for its particular job in life. A dog like this, and his horse, are the Australian stockman's real mates.

Cutting
and the
Calgary
Stampede

Top
Australians are beginning to take a
great interest in Quarter Horses
and their inherent ability for the
American cutting competitions.

Right
Bulldogging at a rodeo in Arizona.
The services of a hazer are
necessary to keep the steer on a
straight course.

Above
Rodeo in New Mexico. One arm
aloft, one hand on the rigging, legs
arching over the shoulders—a
bareback rider who looks at home.

Right
Gail Lougher, daughter of the
founder of the Clover Leaf Stud,
giving a cutting demonstration in
1968 at their first annual horse show
and sale at Murrurundi

Below
The New Zealand champion bull-
dogging when doing the Australian
Circuit. All stock horses are small,
and few rodeo horses are more
than 14·2–15 hands.

The stock horse has been keeping his position so that the rope falls true, and now he starts to take the strain.

A top class Cutting Horse is half a ton of controlled energy—lightning fast both on the straight and on the turn, tough and intelligent above average, and with an uncanny cow-sense that once developed enables it to work without aid of its rider, much like a first-rate Collie dog herding sheep.

The sport of 'Cutting'—bringing an animal out of the drove and keeping it out—stems from normal range work, and is now a popular item in numerous shows and rodeos, particularly in the U.S.A. and Canada. It is just catching on in Australia, and the first Cutting Event took place in May 1968 in Brisbane.

Cattle are gregarious beasts, and it takes a highly trained horse to prevent the steer or heifer from breaking back into the mob. The obvious competitive element in this work turned Cutting first of all into a Sunday afternoon sport for small towns and ranches in the West, and then into a big draw at the larger centres. In 1964 a Canadian Cutting Horse team came to England, their exciting competitions proving immensely popular at the large horse shows where they were put on.

Once the rider has brought his selected steer clear of the herd, he looses the reins, retaining no contact with his mount by bit or neck-reining and the horse takes over. 'Reining' or 'cueing'

the horse in any way is penalized, and the rider usually holds his rein hand out where the judges can see it, with the other on the saddle horn. Some riders give a show without a bridle at all.

The Cutting Horse works unaided, but its rider has to be an accomplished horseman, remaining in perfect balance with his horse so that it is not hampered by his shifting weight during the fast, dramatic stops and turns. Cutting rules impose a big penalty if the steer returns to the herd, and the difficulties of preventing it, and the excitement of the contest as a spectacle, are added to by a couple of hazers (turn-back men) who do all they can to aid the beast in its endeavours.

The Cutting Horse has to demonstrate his ability to out-think and out-manoeuvre the other animal, and they engage in a kind of ritualistic dance. The horse crouches, swaying on his haunches, and lowers his head to fix the steer almost eye to eye, poised to uncoil and follow turn for turn and twist for twist. Sometimes he changes direction in mid-air and foils the steer's attempts to break back with bursts of terrific speed and sudden, dead stops.

A spirited steer gives the horse more scope to exhibit its skill. If the rider wishes to exchange a lethargic beast for another, he retakes control of his horse before signalling the judges by

Below
Hundreds of shows are staged
annually in the U.S. and Canada
where youngsters on Quarter
Horses compete against one
another for handsome awards and
public acclaim

Right
The calf is roped and the horse is
taking the strain. Even a tenth of a
second counts in a calf roping
contest.

raising his reining-hand and placing the
other across his horse's withers.

Training a Cutting Horse is a highly
specialized art, and only a very small
percentage reach the 'top ten', championship class horses being even rarer.
Those that do achieve the top-flights
are extremely valuable, prized above all
by their proud owners.

Any young horse destined for this
work must have a high intelligence, and
an inborn cow-sense that can be developed until he can 'read cattle'. These
innate qualifications are most often
found in Quarter Horses.

The roots of this admirable American
breed lie in the descendants of those
horses, brought to the New World by
the Conquistadores, which escaped to
found the huge, roving herds of mustangs. As the American West was
opened up, many mustangs were

caught and used as cow-ponies. In the
mid-1600s, English settlers along the
eastern coast of North America imported British stallions, among them two
small but fast and sturdy animals called
Janus and Herod. These two proved
exceptionally prepotent in passing on
their special characteristics, and, bred
with the intelligent, tough, working
mustang mares, established a definite
type within a few generations. Experienced selection and interbreeding
furthered this good start, although a
stud book and registry for the breed was
not started until 1941.

Quarter Horses are small, short-
coupled animals with great muscular
strength, particularly of thighs and
quarters. They have brains and quality
to a marked degree, are hardy and
active, and combine above-average
speed over short distances with the re-

markable, inbred sense for working stock. 'Quarter Mile Running Horses' originally competed over the short, rough tracks in Virginia–the distance well suited to these tough sprinters which also enabled their betting public to keep a necessary eye on the jockeys!

There are different strains of this breed, those used for racing being finer and faster than the stock horses. Quarter Horse racing is becoming increasingly popular on the American continent. Stock is now being bred for the sport in Australia, in preparation for racing in a few years' time. A race in New·Mexico, run over 220–240 yards, is today worth around $ 600,000 in prize money. The sprinters squat down in their starting stalls and work up a good foothold for themselves, emerging like shots from a gun and occasionally leaving behind any loose-fitting shoes.

Quarter Horses were first imported into Australia in 1954 by the King Ranch. Thirteen years later the thirty foundation animals of the Clover Leaf Stud arrived at Murrurundi, N.S.W., after a frustrating voyage from America–which lasted many months after quarantine was refused in England because of swamp fever regulations. Quarter Horses from this flourishing stud now frequently exhibit their breed's specialized skills throughout New South Wales and Queensland, and help to promote interest in American stock handling methods.

As a breed these horses are naturally kind and quiet to handle; bucking and shying are unforgivable sins in a stock horse. A well trained animal stands rock still for mounting and dismounting, walks fast, backs quietly and instantly, and keeps up its favourite pace, a

Below
Nothing but the rhythm of his
swinging legs and the grip of one
hand on the rigging keeps the
bareback bronc rider in place for
the requisite eight seconds

Right
Many broncs become more famous
than the riders. Some are really
mean, but not a few quieten down
in seconds directly the buckstrap
is loosened.

smooth lope, for mile upon mile.
Schooled Quarter Horses are exceptionally sensitive, and even a good
rider, used to British riding methods,
may at first find himself all at sea. A
slight shift of his weight, and his horse
will spin round on the proverbial six-
pence, with no apparent sign of ever
stopping again; the merest touch of the
rider's legs, and his horse shoots from
a standstill to a fast canter—but if the
bound throws his weight on to the back
of the saddle or he so much as touches
the animal's mouth, it will obediently
slide to a dead halt, its hocks beneath it
all prepared for the shock of holding a
roped steer!

Races for Quarter Horses are inter-
spersed with those for Thoroughbreds
on the daily programme of the Calgary
Stampede—the toughest, gayest,
noisiest and greatest outdoor show on
earth.

April 1st 1912 was the beginning, when
a lanky American in a black stetson

brought his dream of the 'greatest frontier days celebration the world has ever seen' to Calgary, a fast growing town within sight and smell of the Rockies, set in the heart of the horse and cattle ranching industry of western Canada.

It took time to get the backing, but on August 1st of that year, a big crowd rode in procession through the streets, in the first ever Calgary Stampede Parade.

There were bronc, trick, fancy and Roman Race riders; top rodeo exponents from Mexico; fifty other American top-flighters complete with mounted cowboy band, and hundreds of tough Canadians from Manitoba, Saskatchewan, Alberta and British Columbia—cowboys all, but working men from the ranges, who lacked the tricks and showmanship of the 'professionals'. There were Plains Indians, Sarcees and Blackfoot, Peigans and Bloods, Stonys and Crees, around 2,000 in all, many of whom, as the Mounted Police remem-

bered with some misgiving, had ridden in the Riel Rebellion only twenty-seven years before.

But there was no trouble, and for four days 14,000 enthusiastic spectators thrilled to the sight of internationally famous bronc riders and equally famous buck-jumpers exploding around the arena like fire-crackers, to feats of daring and horsemanship of which they had never dreamed. The show proved a smash hit, and The Calgary Stampede had come to stay.

It rained that second day in 1912, but now it always seems to come hot each year for those nine July days when Calgary is taken over by around 800,000 people, all bent on letting their hair down and returning to the atmosphere and glories of the old great Wild West.

The unofficial Stampede uniform is blue jeans and check shirts for the men, frilly, pioneering-era squaw dresses for the women, and the universal emblem of a cowboy hat, blue, pink, what-you-will, or authentic stetsons for the bow-legged cowboys swaggering by. You can eat a Stampede breakfast on the street, topping up with pancakes and maple syrup; go square dancing to the music of a dozen Western bands; or just drift around in laughing droves, shouting, flirting, drinking as you will.

There are 1,000 or more head of pedigree stock to admire in the exhibition grounds. Sheep and cattle and spindle-legged foals; the towering rounded rumps of Clydesdales lining a long barn; big-muscled Quarter Horses;

Arabians, with their lovely, deer-like heads, and rows of patient cows complying with milking demonstrations.

You can have your fortune told a dozen times, have a go at Bingo, take a chance on anything from a toy teddy-bear to the Pot o' Gold Give-Away, a $ 50,000 gold brick. Try your luck on the rifle-range? Scream your heart out on the space wheels? Eat your fill of sticky cotton-candy, toffee-apples, or mounds of rainbow-striped ice-cream? You can fight your way through the rising dust, the hot, glaring light, past blaring loud-speakers, evading hordes of chocolate-smeared small children who pause in mid-flight to demand a dime, and find yourself by the stands of enchanting Canadian pottery and Indian and Eski-

Left
Certainly not his first try-out at
saddle bronc riding

Right
The Secretary-Treasurer of the
Australian Rough Riders competing in the Open Bronc Ride at
Warwick annual rodeo—with a
horse that understands the art of
sunfishing!

Below
This rider will be lucky if he
manages to stay put!

mo work. There is a moment to gape at
two little ponies treading an old time
threshing machine, and then on to the
Indian Village—with its gay tepees and
the braves in native dress 'on display',
proud and aloof in their total detachment from the surrounding hubbub.

But the biggest draw of all lies in the
Grandstand Enclosure, where world
champions, professionals and ama-
teurs of rodeo, daily risk their lives for
prestige—and the $ 100,000 worth of
prize money.

Out there, beyond the tiers of seats
and the circular race-track, a horse
erupts out of the chute, a coiled spring
of muscle and evil intent. As its forelegs
hit the ground in the first spine-jarring
buck-jump, the rider's blunted spurs

Below
A rough rider at Mount Isa,
Queensland, who looks as though
he may score well

Right
A couple of Australian pickup men
waiting to see if their services are
required at a Queensland rodeo

must be over its shoulders for him to qualify; and throughout the eight seconds he has to stay put, the rake and rhythm of his legs to and fro on the bronc's sides give him balance – and a chance of higher marks if he achieves the 'lick', the full arcing stroke.

The saddle bronc wears no bit. There is a single rope to the rider's hand and he holds his other arm high; he is disqualified if he changes hands, loses a stirrup, or touches horse, rein or saddle with his free hand. The crowd roars, egging him on, and those vital eight seconds can seem a lifetime on top a twisting hunk of horseflesh, as it rears, jack-knifes, kicks and 'sunfishes', finally exploding in a lightning succession of stiff-legged, back-breaking bucks across the arena. And even if the rider survives the time limit his troubles are not over. He still has to get off.

Sometimes he half jumps, half falls, rolling out of the way of the flying hooves. Sometimes a pickup man (a mounted cowboy) races alongside, hauling him on to his own horse's quarters, to bounce perilously around or descend ignominiously over its tail.

Saddle bronc riding is a classic event, only learned through years of experience with rough horses. Most times the horse wins, adding to its reputation; catapulting its rider headlong, it continues a mad solo until driven out of the arena – or until the pickup men manage to loosen the buckstrap, that primer to a bronc's performance that is cinched tightly around its loins.

Another bronc explodes out of the chute, this time unencumbered by saddle or headstall. The taut-faced cowboy spurs even more wildly, the rhythm of his swinging legs all he has to keep his seat close up by his riding hand, clasping the rigging – a suitcase-like handle attached to the surcingle. Once lose the rhythm, straighten your riding arm or slide back from your hand-hold, and you've had it – and the farther back you get on a high-kicking horse, the higher and farther will that mean bunch of bucking ability launch you.

Fancy your prowess on a bucking horse? Then try your luck with a cross-bred Brahma bull, a savage that does everything but turn inside out when you are on top, and attacks you when you hit the ground.

The bulls also charge mounted men, precluding the pickup men, so that your limbs or your life depend on the arena clown – whose baggy pants disguise an artist of speed and courage with a crucial 'bull insight'. And how you pray for his diverting tactics when what you

Previous page
Chaos ensues when the teams get
to work in the Wild Horse Race

Right
Cutting horses work on their own
initiative; this Quarter Horse is
'fixing' the steer and moving with it
in a kind of ritualistic dance

dread happens—when the Brahma bucks you away from your riding hand, and your own weight keeps your gloved fingers fast in the snug handhold that you contrived so carefully with the end of the flat plait looped around the bull's middle. Helpless you hang, dragged around like a lifeless rag-doll until your fist wrenches free, or the clown secures your rescue.

When, like peas from a pod, the chutes start disgorging furious young steers and heifers, each with its determined boy rider aged fifteen or less, you realize where the tough rodeo riders first learned their art. The steers reckon their mission in life is to make beef on the hoof, not act as ridden broncs, and with the crowd yelling its delight and the dust rising in clouds, they burst around the arena, discharging boys in all directions in a tangle of arms and legs and remarkably blue language.

Here comes a stock horse, breaking through the barrier as though it were the sound one, racing after a calf that left an opposite chute some seconds earlier. The calf may weave and jink but the horse closes quickly, steadily, to keep a length behind and a fraction to one side, allowing for its rider's clean throw of the lariat. The noose falls true, the horse slides to a stop, bracing against the weight and propelling the roper down his tautened lariat towards his objective as he comes out of his saddle running. Tenths of a second count, and he throws his calf, wrapping three legs with a soft 'pigging string', and flings his hands high to signal completion; but the tie must hold six seconds, and even at this triumphant moment the calf may be trotting nonchalantly away in the background, ac-

companied by the spectators' jeers.

Try leaning from the back of a galloping horse to snatch a steer's right horn, tucking it snugly into the crook of your right elbow, and pushing down on the other horn with your free hand while your horse veers off left without you. That is steer wrestling, and you dig your forward thrusting heels in at an angle in a desperate attempt to throw the twenty hundredweight of racing, reluctant beef in a faster time than any other competitor.

No? Well, can you milk a cow? There is a mounted range rider needing a milker on foot to complete his team. He will rope you a cow from among the mob of wild bossies waiting to be turned loose from the chutes. She has never been handled, let alone milked before. She may drag your anchor man halfway down the arena before you catch up, but all you have to do is to collect two inches of her milk in a small bottle, and then bow-leg it like hell, high heels, spurs, milk and all, back to the judges' stand.

If that does not appeal then team up for the Wild Horse Race contest. Make one of the three men assigned to each of the sixteen outlaws that are spilled down the runways into the chutes. As the chute gates are thrown wide they will erupt into the arena, each trailing a sixteen-foot rope from its halter. Each team has first to halt its horse, anchor it with one man, saddle and cinch it, and leave the third team member to race it to the pickup chute. Easy money you say? Maybe—if any of those horses had ever known a man's hand before.

Then as the heat of the day stills to a golden evening, as the Canadian flag wilts against its pole and the sweat-dripping pickup horses droop, caked

with dust to their ears, an added air of expectancy begins to build up and expand. The endless betting grows to more feverish heights. Dark faces shaded by greasy hat-brims take on a new animation, and members of every race and creed from neat, precise Frenchmen to long-haired British girls, from swarthy Indians padding through the dust on bare, leathery soles to American families out on the spree, all arrive to swell the crowds around the central arena. It is time for the heats of the Rangeland Derby, the maddest, most dangerous form of racing in the world.

These chuck wagon races stem from when, the round-up completed, the cowboys headed a bunch of round-up wagons back across the prairie in a wild dash for town. Organized races were first included in the Stampede in 1923.

The wagons are stripped to bare essentials, so light that the drivers bounce like peas as they canter their teams up and down before the start, waving and shouting to friends in the crowd despite the effort of controlling four over excited, racing-fit Thoroughbred horses, all decked out in gay red or yellow harness.

Each wagon has four outriders attached. They stand in moody clumps, shirt-tails hanging from their pants and nervous tension proclaiming the difficulties of their role in the event; then they load their own particular wagon in a flash with pole, canvas and a cooking stove, mount their horses and set off in pursuit, to remain on station flanking the swaying vehicles.

Four outfits make up each heat, and for the start they take up places in the centre field, the teams dancing and prancing, their ears flicking to and fro. The signal goes. Tents, stoves and poles thump into the wagons, the drivers fling their teams in a figure of eight round the marking barrels, then head lickety-split for the race track – while the outriders leap desperately for the backs of their whirling, frenzied horses. There is a thunder of hooves and the wagons lurch from side to side. An outrider's horse flies by, its rider prone and making frantic attempts to swing his leg over the saddle. Into the home straight they come now, the creaking wagons flat out, wobbling wheels converging within inches of each other, swearing drivers glancing over their shoulders as they stand up, yelling at their teams; and the horses, ears flat, strain every muscle.

They are through the finish! A great audible sigh goes up, and the drivers cry 'Whoa! Whoa!' as they wrench back on teams still keen for another circuit; more outriders are trailing, rolling in their saddles, black with dust; then the horse teams go prancing sideways back to the barn, with wide eyes and laboured snorts, to the accompaniment of the crowd's banter at the 'also rans'.

The sun has gone, the sideshows are outlined in lights, red and green and yellow; there is a queue to see the world's fattest lady and the alligator woman; people swoop screaming on the thundering shoots of the big dipper, shout hysterically as their necks crack on the giant whip. Later come the fireworks, shattering the night sky into scintillating fragments of colour. When the last squib dies, laughing crowds drift slowly through the hushed streets, back to bed and sleep to renew their energies for the excitements of the next day at the greatest outdoor show on earth, the Calgary Stampede.

Chuck wagon racing at Calgary Stampede

POLO
PONIES

Previous page
Prince Philip (dark jersey) riding
off an opponent with all the
forceful determination that
characterizes his game

Right
A Persian miniature of the sixteenth century depicts a spotted
horse playing polo. The attractive
spotted colouring has been prized
all over the world for centuries.

Far right
The art of an Isfahan craftsman
shows that even in the days of Shah
Abbas, polo sticks were much the
same and Persian horses just as
fiery as they are today

Shah Abbas climbed the narrow stairway of his palace, the Ali Qapu, to a high terrace. The roof was supported by tall wooden pillars, the warm air flower-scented, and on the other three sides of the square laid out below rose the domes and slender minarets that continue to form Isfahan's unforgettable skyline. The gold-patterned dome of the exquisite Sheikh Luftol'ah Mosque glistened in the sun, and the brilliant blue and turquoise tilework of the Shah Mosque stood out over all.

The Shah looked down to that space, seven times larger than St. Mark's Piazza, which he had planned as a place of assembly and sport for the citizens of Isfahan, his capital city. Sometimes there would be nobles jousting on horseback, or lions combating fierce bulls. Sometimes skilled horsemen galloped by, turning in their saddles to shoot with bows and arrows at a golden bowl suspended on a high pole. On that particular day the Shah's courtiers were playing polo.

That game took place more than 300 years ago. Today a sheet of ornamental water reflects the pillars of the Ali Qapu, and the maidan is laid out with beds of sweet-smelling flowers; but the same stone goal posts still stand, and contemporary miniatures depict those players of long ago using curiously modern polo sticks.

Even in the time of Shah Abbas polo was a very ancient game. Originating in Persia and Northern India, it was first played on any flat ground or up and down a wide village street, governed by local rules and with an unlimited number of players. A similar game 'without boundaries' and the site often a rocky mountain slope, still takes place in parts of Asia with the players mounted on small, active native ponies.

Polo remains a popular game in Iran, and in 1968 a visiting British team was entertained with good sport and the characteristic and unforgettable Persian hospitality.

In 1869 some home-based officers of the 11th Hussars read of 'hockey on horseback' being played in India with eight a side. The idea appealed, but sticks with bent heads, billiard balls and a few uncomprehending and uncooperative Army chargers, turned that first game of British polo into an indescribable melée! Soon, however, ponies were being brought over from Ireland, the height limit set first at 14 hands, then at 14·2, proper rules were drawn up, and the players reduced to the modern teams of four.

The game took some years to become firmly established, but in India polo quickly became as popular with British officers as the troops' own favourite football, and Arabian horses proved their agile worth. Although Arabians are nowadays outclassed in high-goal polo, where Thoroughbred or Argentine ponies of horse size are used, they are still admirable for the game in many countries. The team of the Royal Highland Fusiliers discovered this when they went to Morocco and had the pick of the Arabian stallions which were used as polo ponies by their adversaries Le Garde Royale, stationed in Rabat.

The height limit for ponies was abolished after the First World War. As bigger animals were used, the smaller ponies could not compete with their speed and weight, and the polo 'pony'

became a horse, sometimes of sixteen hands. Nowadays few genuine ponies are played in any but the lowest grade games. With the use of Thoroughbreds polo has become much faster. But although a top-class 'pony' has still to be as well schooled as before, length and accuracy of strokes to some extent supplant the finesse and skilful stick-work which was required when polo 'ponies' were of a size to merit the name.

Many top-notch British and American ponies, and players, come from the Argentine. The ponies are the offspring of Thoroughbreds crossed with Criollo mares–those admirable, tough descendants of Spanish and Portuguese horses brought to South America by the Conquistadores. Criollos and their variations are the working cattle horses of the Argentine and other South American countries, and show an in-bred aptitude for the stops, accelerations, twists and turns required both on the ranch and on the polo ground. And while there is nothing to better a first-class Thoroughbred pony, their hot temperaments often make them less suitable for the game than the slightly slower but more equable Argentine animals.

Prince Charles' first polo pony was an Argentine, a well-versed elderly mare called San Quanina given him by his father. With the equally aged and wise Sombra, a present from Lord Cowdray, the Prince began playing at the age of seventeen.

As a child Prince Charles enjoyed riding the various small ponies belong-ing at one time and another to him and

Princess Anne. But he never quite de-veloped his sister's enthusiasm for the sport, and once at boarding school other occupations superseded riding, until the exciting attractions of polo proved irresistible. Now Prince Charles enjoys the game as much as Prince Philip. He has inherited the same natural eye for a ball and shows increas-ingly promising form. The speed of polo, plus its toughness and the very real spice of danger appeal to both father and son, but Prince Charles is too aware of his ponies as personalities to provide quite the same forceful thrust, the 100 per cent will to win that characterizes Prince Philip's play.

Prince Philip has the above average handicap rating of five goals (handicaps range from minus two up to ten–an ex-ceptional figure) and captains the well-known Windsor Park side whenever he can spare the time. He plays regularly at Smith's Lawn in the Great Park where the Queen and Princess Anne enjoy watching, and where the game some-times includes Prince Charles and Prince William of Gloucester.

Prince Charles' three or four ponies are kept at Windsor in the royal mews and adjacent to the compact range of stabling called Prince Philip's Yard which houses his father's animals. These ponies belonging to Prince Philip include all grades, ranging from novices playing their first season of slow polo to the most experienced and valuable. A number are Argentine ponies, both lightweights and the heavier type. One of the best known of the many Thoroughbreds was Betaway,

The melee   E. Giberne

a granddaughter of the Derby winner Hyperion, and renowned for her exceptional speed before she was retired to stud. The Queen is interested in breeding a few polo ponies, and occasionally one is included in Prince Philip's string.

Like the majority of polo ponies, those at Windsor are looked after by girl grooms, although the initial schooling, a highly skilled job, is done by experts. It may take up to two years to produce a fully trained pony.

The interest of attending matches in different parts of England, as well as the chance of travelling abroad, is attached to the job of girl groom to polo ponies. But the work is hard, the hours are long and include weekends, when matches are normally played. The girls have to be good riders, capable of coping with highly-strung, extremely valuable animals; and since polo ponies are roughed off, running out through the winter from the end of each season until the end of the following February, exercising when they first come in sometimes contains an element of rodeo!

Each girl is normally responsible for two ponies. This includes grooming, feeding, trimming, tack-cleaning and mucking out, in addition to the gradually stepped-up programme of exercise and schooling. The ponies require from an hour to an hour and a half on grass or the soft tan of an indoor school, mostly at the canter, and on every day throughout the season except when they are playing. The job of groom to polo ponies calls for a dedicated approach, yet the majority of the girls return year after year for this seasonal work and take the greatest pride in the prowess of their charges.

Some of the most famous British polo grounds were lost for ever during the Second World War, but Malta held a tournament in 1968 to celebrate playing on the same ground for the past 100 years. What is now one of the most beautiful grounds in the world was until a short while ago a waste of Spanish sand dunes. Now it is possible to play polo there close by the dancing sea with mountains looming up in the background, the misty coast of Africa within sight, and the dark mass of the Rock of Gibraltar rearing to the west.

Polo is an international game but today's great playing centres are the U.S.A. and the Argentine. It seemed unlikely that the game would revive in England after the Second World War. Ponies were scarce, and at top levels polo is the world's most expensive game, but largely owing to Lord Cow-

dray's efforts it not only restarted but is growing in popularity. High-goal polo remains the province of the wealthy and of those regiments that field polo teams, but more modest clubs are springing up around the country, and the Pony Club holds an annual polo tournament of increasing importance.

Ponies worth thousands of pounds are necessary for top standards, but almost any horse or pony can be schooled for slow polo in a relatively short space of time—and in addition to its more normal role in life. Also trained ponies which are aged or too slow can be bought relatively cheaply, and these are invaluable for the novice player.

When Australia changed over from afternoon to evening racing under lights, harness horse racing became a major sport pulling in thousands of spectators and big prize money. Many of the horses have the blood of champion American strains. This is a pacer, the fore and hind leg on one side moving in the same direction, whereas a trotter's fore leg moves in unison with its opposite hind leg. The pacing 'harness' restrains the horse from breaking the pace.

Trotters
& Pacers

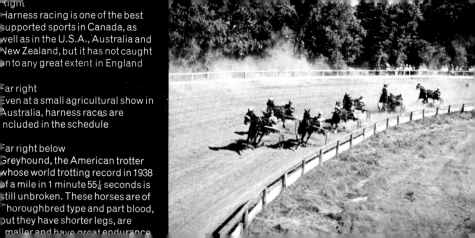

Right
Harness racing is one of the best supported sports in Canada, as well as in the U.S.A., Australia and New Zealand, but it has not caught on to any great extent in England

Far right
Even at a small agricultural show in Australia, harness races are included in the schedule

Far right below
Greyhound, the American trotter whose world trotting record in 1938 of a mile in 1 minute 55¼ seconds is still unbroken. These horses are of thoroughbred type and part blood, but they have shorter legs, are smaller and have great endurance

Below
Canadian pacers demonstrating
what is now usually an artificial
gait. During the Middle Ages,
amblers as they were then called
were much prized as riding horses
for their smooth and gliding motion.

Bottom
Harness racing with a difference:
horse-drawn sledges racing
through the snow on an ice-bound
lake at Kitzbuhel, Austria

Far right
Racing with four-wheeled sulkies
at Norwood, Ontario

Eventing
Jumping
Circus &
Haute Ecole

Previous page
Even the most novice cross-country course in an event will include water—to jump into or over, or to go through. Unless horses are accustomed to dealing with this hazard they often refuse to have anything to do with it.

Right
The training of these Arabian Liberty horses is founded on the constant size of the circus ring

Below
The movements required of Liberty horses are all based on a horse's natural leaps and bounds, but in case of strained tendons they are not worked on their hind legs until mature

Far right
Members of the famous Schumann family with some of their high school horses.

In our sophisticated age the circus is a declining form of entertainment, and even those shows that remain rely more on human than on equine acts.

One reason for its lessening popularity is the belief that circus animals are trained by cruelty. There are always exceptions, but no cowed or frightened horse would show the fine condition and joie de vivre exhibited by those belonging to the large circuses. The majority of animals are born 'show offs', and the fattest old pony, given an appreciative audience, enjoys displaying those same leaps and bounds on which equine circus acts are based. Many animals used to performing in public pine if deprived of their spotlights and audiences.

Before the sixteenth century there was a horse carrying out 'tumbling and apish tricks wherewith he got his living'; and later another, called Morocco, was exhibited before crowded galleries in the courtyard of the Belle Sauvage on Ludgate Hill, and became famous for an act that included a bizarre dance called the Canaries.

Philip Astley, ex-Sergeant Major of the 15th Light Dragoons and a superb horseman, unwittingly founded the British circus. He failed with a riding school intended to revive the aristocratic traditions of indoor horsemanship but through an excellent advertising campaign which embodied exhibitions of trick riding, found himself instead the proprietor of a successful circus. He and his horses performed daring feats, put on to the accompaniment of Mrs. Astley beating a drum.

In Paris during the nineteenth century it became as fashionable to visit the stables of the Cirque d'Eté, as the coulisses of the Opéra. Under Baucher the artistry of haute école took pride of place over pure trick riding, and only in Victorian London was the circus considered an amusement solely for children.

This outlook changed when each Christmas for many years before and

Right
The serving members of the Cadre Noir, chosen from the élite of cavalry riders, are all superb horsemen

Far right
The Spanish riding school Quadrille performed by twelve white Lipizzaners is almost like a ballet

Far right below
At the Spanish school in Vienna only Lipizzaner stallions are used to perform haute école movements such as this levade

after the Second World War, Bertram Mills collected together in London the best of the world's circus acts. Pimpo the clown became a tradition, and audiences gasped at the perilous exploits of riders like the Australian Wirths, or feasted their eyes on the entrancing displays by Schumann's Liberty horses.

There are three main categories of circus horse. Rosinbacks are heavy horses, broad quartered for the acrobats to leap to stand upon them, with imperturbable natures and the willingness to keep up a smooth, slow canter round the ring. High school or dancing horses are superbly trained, and ridden by accomplished horsemen to exhibit many of the classical and some less orthodox movements of haute école. Liberty horses perform in groups, the standard of training, the lighting, music and the beauty of the horses and their trappings all adding to the spectacular effect. Like all animal circus acts the schooling of Liberty horses is based on

the never varying size of the ring. Each horse knows its name and is immediately responsive to it. They are 'cued' verbally, by the position the trainer takes up in the ring, and by indications of his long whip which is never used for punishment.

Circus horses are trained with patience, but the period does not extend to the five years or so which are lavished on a Lipizzaner stallion before it reaches the perfection demanded for the display of haute école at the Spanish Riding School in Vienna. Completed in 1735, the lovely baroque building was first used to give cavalry instruction to the young sons of Court nobles—a form of training that developed into haute école, the uncorrupted interpretation of the highest art of classical riding.

The horses are white Lipizzaners, a breed derived from Spanish Andalusians with other blood, including Arabian, introduced through the years. They show recognizably different

strains, produced by selective and line breeding, but any stallion chosen for the Spanish School must conform to the high standards of beauty, presence, strength and stamina allied to docility and intelligence.

The men who school these horses undergo an arduous instruction themselves, and it takes ten years to become a Bereiter, fully qualified to train a stallion.

Many of the breathtaking, superbly controlled movements of haute école are directly derived from cavalry exercises, employed during the Middle Ages to terrify and disperse unmounted troops. Unsuspecting infantry must have been more than disconcerted to see horses bounding towards them on their hind legs as in the Courbette. The Capriole, when the horse leaps in the air, lashing out with its hind legs at the same time, must have provided wonderful protection for any mounted knight besieged from both before and behind.

The classical 'airs' are also taught at

Right
The piaffer, or trot on the spot, performed by a German Holsteiner, a breed with the quiet temperament necessary for dressage and haute école

Below
A good rider has a seat independent of reins or stirrups. Exercises on the lunge, when the trainer controls the horse, are excellent at any stage of horsemanship, even for Olympic riders such as Jeremy Beale.

Far right
Stroller is only a pony in size but he and his young owner Marion Coakes have beaten most of the show jumping horses—and won the silver medal for show jumping at the Mexico Olympics

the highest levels at Saumur, the famous French Cavalry School formed in 1814 from the pre-revolutionary cavalry of the French royal household and the Versailles civilian school of equitation. Saumur combined past and present glories in 1945 to become the School of Instruction of the Armoured Corps and the Cavalry, and despite mechanization all officers and many NCOs of the Armoured Corps take a short course of riding.

They are instructed by members of the Cadre Noir, so named from the colour of their uniform, superb horsemen all, chosen from the élite of cavalry riders. The course is designed to produce riders with some knowledge of race-riding, and competent to compete in show jumping and combined training events. There is also a refresher course, and the ten-month-long Cours de Perfectionnement d'Equestre which may yield one or two possible future recruits for the Cadre Noir.

In addition to their work as instructors, the twelve serving members of the Cadre Noir ride in amateur races and compete at shows and events all over France, the most experienced taking part in top level dressage competitions. Once a week they work together in a magnificent public performance of collective dressage, demonstrating the supple obedience of the big Thoroughbreds and Anglo-Arabs they ride—horses of great quality and presence that are also a delight to watch outside the manège, galloping over fences. The morning ends with the unforgettable Reprise des Sauteurs when the Cadre Noir, riding short-striding little Norman horses, display the haute école 'airs above the ground' at the speed and with

the quick action of a medieval battle.

There are wonderful facilities for training at Saumur. At Breil on the outskirts of the town forty acres of parkland contain everything from a miniature race track to natural show jumping obstacles such as banks and water. Four miles away at Verrie a steeplechase course is surrounded by acres of woods with miles of galloping tracks and fences, and in the hillier parts there is terrain and every possible solid type of fence for schooling three-day event riders and horses.

The 1968 Olympic three-day-event individual gold medallist, Jean-Jacques Guyon, was able to take full advantage of these training areas when he served in the Cadre Noir as Adjutant-chef.

Eventing is the youngest of the equestrian sports, yearly growing in popularity with both competitors and spectators.

An event horse has to be active in his paces and both supple and obedient to gain good marks in the dressage phase of a horse trial or one-day event. He has to be courageous and fit to cope with the many different obstacles encountered on the cross-country course, and versatile enough to jump a round of show fences in the third phase. Three-day events are considerably more arduous, and essentially different competitions. For these the horse has to possess even more speed for the additional steeplechase course, and great stamina to complete the miles of roads and tracks that follow on, before embarking on the cross-country.

An Olympic three-day event is the stiffest possible test of both horse and rider, with the additional difficulties presented by the different climate and conditions of the chosen venue.

Experience is essential, and the Australians demonstrated their fine horsemanship by coming third in 1968 at Mexico, despite riding young horses of only six years old. At the other end of the scale, the Australian No. 4 rider, Bill Roycroft (a gold medallist at Rome in 1960) and the British Major Allhusen, winner of the individual silver at Mexico, are both well over fifty! With the exception of an East German horse, the Russian stallions had it all their own way in the dressage phase, but lacked experience when it came to jumping across country.

Other essential qualities are needed in this form of competition. The emphasis is on the team in this Olympic event, and since both team and individual awards are contested at the same time, the rider capable of performing as an unselfish team member is more likely to be selected than a brilliant individualist. Lack of team spirit contributed to the British failure in the 1964 Tokyo Olympics, just as surely as its presence gained the team a gold medal for Great Britain at Mexico in 1968.

Fitness is the greatest necessity of all. The hot sun and humid conditions took more toll at Mexico than either the altitude, or the tropical storm that eventually turned streams on the cross-country course into torrents strong enough to roll a horse over and left only the marker flags at two fences visible above the surrounding water. The storms also turned the arena for the show jumping phase into a quagmire. Tired horses could not possibly cope with either the heat or the going. The British horses – and the American horses, which came second – were in wonderful hard condition, and had all been well hunted. The British horses are also practised in the art of jumping hunt fences out of hock-deep, sticky British mud.

The going also had a bearing on the result of the show jumping for the Grand Prix des Nations in the Olympic Stadium in Mexico. Four days previously Bill Steinkraus had jumped Snowbound to victory for the U.S.A., and Marion Coakes, riding the little marvel Stroller, had taken the silver medal for Great Britain. Then Snowbound went lame, and there seemed good reason to think the British team could win the Prix des Nations.

But horses are not machines, the distances between combination and other fences proved particularly difficult, and the ground was both holding and slippery. The course was formidable, there was not a single clear round, and horses

as good even as Italy's Doneraile, the Australian Bonvale (which was fourth at Tokyo) and the French Quo Vadis, all had scores of over twenty faults. Only the British Mister Softee ridden by David Broome, the Canadian horse The Immigrant, Enigk for Germany, and the American San Lucas ridden by Frank Chapot, achieved respectable scores in the first round. Finally the gold medal went to Canada, the silver to France, and Germany took the bronze.

Show jumping was first included in the Olympic Games in 1912. Until the eighteenth century the ability of horses to jump anything much higher than small banks and ditches had never really been considered. It was an unnecessary art until common land was enclosed. Then the foxhunters had to learn to leap hedges to continue their sport and horsemen found a new thrill attached to riding.

In England 'lepping' shows were first held around the beginning of the century. These were dull affairs, with competitors jumping a single three-foot-six-inch rail, which was raised six inches each round, with three successive displacements bringing elimination. Lady competitors rode side-saddle, and the horses were mostly small light-boned hacks with docked tails. Very different from the big quality show jumpers of today, which are usually half or three-quarter bred and extremely expensive, adding to the very high overall costs of the sport.

Television brings all the excitement of modern show jumping even into the homes of people not otherwise interested in horses, and the names of the internationally famous show jumpers and their riders are household words. The top-flighters fly their horses to-compete all over the world. New York, Toronto, Sydney, Geneva, Dublin, Madrid, Rotterdam, Rome and many other cities hold celebrated annual jumping shows. The jumpers compete at the Sports Club at Casablanca; Russian competitors jump for coveted medals in the Moscow Hippodrome; there is good jumping to be seen at the three-day Agricultural Show in Bermuda. In addition to the spate of show jumping competitions that take place all over Britain during the summer, indoor jumping, as in the States and Canada, is becoming a popular winter sport. At Hickstead the Jumping Derby is held. This outdoor arena is the Mecca for all show jumping experts; the courses are some of the most difficult in the world, numbers of the fences are permanent features, and a notorious bank each

Top left
Fiery Persian horses are not easy to train for jumping, but the Officer Commanding the Imperial Guard is an expert.

Centre left
The Jordanian Royal Guard have formed a successful show jumping team. Like most Arabian horses, their show jumpers tend to take their fences with a flat back and high held head.

Bottom left
Sergeant Jones riding The Poacher for Britain in the three-day event at the Mexico Olympics

Below
Members of the U.S.A. 1968 Olympics team jumping down into water. The cross-country phase of a horse trial or three-day event requires a lot of practice.

Most show jumping courses include combination fences—precision jumps requiring plenty of impulsion to get horse and rider safely over the two or three elements that make up the fence. Here David Broome is coming safely out of one such hazard with Top of the Morning II.

year takes its toll. Every October, the crowds that appreciate the varied programme at the Horse of the Year Show are stirred anew by the Puissance horses—those giants of high jumping that tackle a grim grey wall which may sometimes rise to more than seven feet high.

Jumping is an indispensable ingredient of most shows, but the breed and showing classes are equally important. In Britain the show animal should be a model of its breed or type, and in ridden classes the skilled exhibitor can do much to emphasize his horse's good points of carriage, action and training. Show hacks must demonstrate elegance and obedience of a high order, but because they are produced more quickly for the show ring nowadays, few modern hacks aspire to the polished performances of past years.

Australian showing classes approximate to those in England, although they are slightly less formal, conventional dress giving way to the comfort of jodhpurs, tweed jackets and felt 'Robin Hood' hats. High-class Arabian horses take the field at the Rand Easter Show at Johannesburg, and at Kimberley in South Africa. And despite the nuclear age Ireland remains a country of horses and horsemen. To own the Champion Hunter at the famous Royal Dublin, is still the highest ambition of every Irish sportsman.

American Hunter classes can prove puzzling to the uninitiated. An amateur member of a recognized American hunt can enter for the Corinthian Hunter class. His horse's performance and conformation will earn a percentage of marks, but the rider can lose up to fifteen per cent if he forgets to have sandwiches in his sandwich case, or if his horse is wearing a buckled-in instead of a sewn-in bit.

Looks will get a novice hunter nowhere in the First Year Working Hunter class, but he must keep up a steady pace over a course of eight three-foot-six-inch fences, correctly arching neck and back as he jumps. He must take off calmly from the correct distance, for such obstacles as a 'chicken coop'. These are solid wooden box affairs that, fitted over the wire fences, are an aid to hunting some parts of the American countryside.

The conformation of the Working Hunter Under Saddle does not matter. unless it affects his 'way of going'—and that is very different from the active, balanced action required in England. Ridden usually in a snaffle on a loose rein, he carries his head low, relaxed until he lacks any semblance of impulsion. But faced with a four-foot fence, the American Working Hunter tackles it smoothly and calmly, with an enviable and effortless ease. Looks do count in

some Hunter classes, but the horses are first selected on their jumping ability. They are shown 'in hand' in Model Classes like British young stock, but the American hunters can be of any age.

For sheer excitement there is no class or show in the world to compete with the Moroccan Fantasia or Powder Play.

To celebrate the King's presence or a feast day the Moroccan tribesmen leave their camel herds and ride in, several thousand strong, from the stony wastelands of the desert, through light so clear that distances seem immense. A village may be their destination, or they may pitch their tents outside the pink-tinted walls of Marrakesh, hobbling their horses in the shadow of the Qutubiya mosque, the high minaret pointing a dark finger against the flaming skies of sunset.

With daylight the tribesmen muster, perhaps a thousand at a time, in a big arena facing the royal tents. They spring to their saddles, clumsy, high-pommelled affairs with square stirrups, the red Moroccan leather sometimes beautifully decorated or covered in wool cloths worked in brilliant colours. Each rider carries a 'mokkala'—a long single-barrelled rifle, the stock inlaid with ivory or silver—and as the horses come together in a wavering line there is a sudden shout. The plunging ani-

Top
William Steinkraus, riding his well-known horse Snowbound, won the gold medal for the U.S.A. at the 1968 Olympics

Above
Tropical storms turned the tough cross-country course at the Mexico Olympics into a nightmare of overflowing rivers and floods. Norman Elder of the Canadian team came to grief.

At the height of the Moroccan Fantasia, the riders stand in the stirrups and brandish their mokkalas above their heads

mals dash forward, hooves thunder, the crowd yells and the riders stand in their stirrups, waving their mokkalas above their heads. Full gallop they come, sweeping towards the royal recipients of the final salute, when at another shout the rifles are discharged into the air, the riders check their racing horses back on to their haunches and ride back to start again.

Hannibal's Numidian cavalry first perfected the riding part of this difficult manoeuvre, checking their galloping horses without the aid of bridles. The Arabs later adopted the same exercise, their horses controlled by the 'jakama', the single-roped camel halter with which many Bedouin ride today. And this jakama, called 'Jaquima', was introduced by the Conquistadores into the New World, to become the well-known American bitless bridle, the Hackamore.

The Moroccan Powder Play horses are of Barb blood, an ancient breed now little known outside Africa but possessed of much the same endurance and stamina as Arabians—two of the qualities that have made Arabian horses famous above all other breeds for covering immense distances. Soon after the First World War some pure-bred Arabians, each carrying thirteen stone, covered sixty miles in five consecutive days. This breed, and animals containing a percentage of Arabian

blood, are particularly successful in the popular sport of endurance or long-distance riding.

These events are not races, although a minimum speed is required to gain an award. In Britain distances vary from twenty miles for junior Pony Clubbers, to the seventy-five miles in two days of the championship, the Golden Horse-shoe, for which riders have to qualify.

The course for the 100-mile Australian ride, for the Tom Quilty Gold Cup, leads up to and through the Blue Mountains, with a total haul of more than 10,000 feet. In California the Western States Ride for the Tevis Cup is the same length, over the rough, precipitous terrain of the original Indian route from the Cali-

fornian gold mines to Nevada. The riders have to tackle hazards like the notorious Cougar Rock with a sheer drop to either hand; it is a toss-up whether to lead one's horse or hang on to his tail and let him show the way.

On rides like these competitors have to carry food for rider and horse, and water their animals where they can. The horses have to pass stringent veterin-ary tests at various check points along the route, with another for the finalists. The whole test is principally one of horsemanship, needing a lot of experi-enced hard work and correct feeding to get a horse fit enough to enter for a long-distance ride.

Left
The Portman Hounds moving off to draw the first covert

Below
On the wide open spaces of Exmoor there is little to jump other than streams. Horses need stamina and sure-footedness rather than jumping ability, and moorland farmers sometimes follow the hunt on sturdy little Exmoor ponies.

Hunting

Left
The hunt only crosses farm land at the goodwill of the farmer. Horses in numbers can do a great deal of damage, and followers must be prepared to obey the fieldmaster.

Right
Hunting mouflon in Iran, the author and her husband rode two royal horses deep into the vast acreage of the hunting preserves, among the foothills and precipitous slopes of the Elburz range

Below
Huntsman of the Dartmoor Foxhounds, enjoying a stirrup cup at a meet in South Devon

Driving
& Harness
Horses

Previous page
Hunter type horses are often driven in modern coaches

Right
The Irish State Coach is one of the splendid carriages housed in the Royal Mews at Buckingham Palace. Used at the State Opening of Parliament and on other occasions, the coach is drawn by six Windsor Greys controlled by postillions riding the nearside horses.

Far right
Hackney horses at a meet of the Four in Hand Club in Hyde Park. Note the docked tails, tight bearing reins, and the spotted dog which should be trotting between the wheels.

Right below
Driving classes are becoming more popular at Horse Shows

Before wheels were invented several thousands of years ago, horses, oxen and donkeys were used as pack animals, and packhorses were still indispensable in the nineteenth century. When solid wooden wheels, hewn from a tree trunk, were attached loosely to the axle of a sledge, man had his first cart, and trained oxen to draw it.

Solid wheels are liable to split, but stronger wheels were soon being made by means of spokes stuck into a hub and an outer rim – fashioned in much the same way as that employed by one of the few remaining wheelwrights of today.

Carriages arrived during the reign of Queen Elizabeth I, but they were costly and reserved strictly for the aristocracy. They were tunnel-shaped 'luxuries', drawn by three or four heavy horses controlled by postillions. Tapestry lined but with supporting beams resting on the axles, the cumbersome conveyances jolted and bounded over the appalling ruts, and the majority of the people continued to ride horses.

Although there were hackney coaches for hire in London in 1636 – and 'the earth trembled and shook and the casements went shatter-tatter from the trembling din' – all vehicles continued to be drawn by teams of heavy horses or ponderous Flemish. By the time Telford and Macadam were constructing the first good roads since the Roman

occupation, a less heavy type of coach horse, of Spanish blood, was in general use. When a coach builder invented those elliptical springs still used today, yet lighter vehicles were used with lighter horses, and the traffic began to accelerate. Stage and mail coaches ran regularly from 1786, and when the copses were ploughed that formerly harboured highwaymen, greater safety was added to speedier travel.

During the nineteenth century sturdy American Concord coaches were taken to Australia. Harnessed with relays of Walers they provided transport and carried mail, proving almost indestructible even under the extremely rough conditions of the outback. The promoting company was not so successful in South Africa but the Concords, taken over and rechristened Zeederburg Coaches, played no small part in subsequent Cape history. Owing to the scourge of horse sickness, they were often pulled by mules.

In England the railways killed the short-lived stage and mail coach era, but for many years horse-drawn omnibuses and trams, hansom cabs, 'Growlers', tradesmen's turnouts and heavy drays, vied with the elegant carriages of the wealthy to choke the busy streets.

All kinds of horses from hunters to hackneys were used with this miscellany of vehicles. Cleveland Bays, des-

cended from the old Chapman's Horse of the Yorkshire Dales, were favourites. And crossed with Thoroughbreds they produced the handsome Yorkshire Coach Horses that were so popular with the fashionable up to the First World War.

Even in the middle 1930s much of the bread, groceries and coal was still delivered by horse and cart in country districts, and in towns the milkman's horse has not long been superseded. But with the advent of the 'horseless carriages', the carriage horses almost disappeared, except for those teams still driven by people who delight in preserving some of the dash and elegance of a bygone age.

The Coaching Club, formed in 1871 with fifty members, was originated by a Lt. Colonel Henry Armytage, and a Mr. Goddard who had never driven a coach in his life. The driving of four horses as a private pastime had already been given a fillip by an earlier Society, the exclusive, closed-shop Four in Hand Club of 1856. And at the Coaching Club's first meeting, twenty-two coaches with magnificent teams and complete with passengers, assembled at Marble Arch under the eagle eye of the then Prince of Wales, and clattered off in convoy to Greenwich, to dine at the Trafalgar.

At meets held in 1875 and 1877 the Prince of Wales was on the box seat of

the Duke of Beaufort's coach. On June 2nd 1894, a record thirty-nine private coaches met at the Magazine, Hyde Park, to drive to Hurlingham Club for lunch. That same year the Club sponsored 'the first and only' meet of road coaches. Twenty years previously 120 private and regimental four in hands, all members of either the Coaching or the Four in Hand Club, had bowled down to Ascot races together for the Gold Cup.

There are about thirty-five members of the Coaching Club still operative, all of whom are or have been coachmen (in the purest sense), capable of handling a team and turning out resplendent in the Club coat of blue melton cloth worn with a buff waistcoat.

At the Kladruby Stud Farm in Czechoslovakia, they sometimes drive ten Kladrubers in a team – fine white horses, larger than Lipizzaners, bred from one of the oldest strains in Europe. And the same number of Hanoverian stallions are driven during the annual exhibition given at the German State Stud at Celle.

Driving a four in hand does not entail quite the same number of problems, but is still a fine art. The good coachman sorts out what appears to the uninitia-

ted as a maze of reins, and knows with which horse his fingers are conversing. He makes sure his team remains 'in draught' as and when required, with each horse pulling its weight, and is quick to realize when a leader is forging ahead too fast, or when a wheeler is idling. He knows that 'dropping his hands' to an exuberant team on starting will settle them more quickly than pulling at them. The good coachman is certainly alive to the fact that four-wheel-brakes cannot be applied to a team of horses – and there may even be tricky moments when the traffic lights go red as the leaders arrive, and there may be nothing for it but to let them carry on!

Breaking the pole (the timber between the wheelers) is unpleasant and can be dangerous, and is easily done with young, green horses that whip round unexpectedly. Losing a bridle is less usual, but equally hazardous. It happened to one of the leaders of a team of Windsor Greys, sent to meet Queen Elizabeth II at Edinburgh station, at the time when only the wheelers wore bearing reins. All the State Harness is very heavy and impossible to alter for each

Left
Kladrubers, fine horses larger
than Lipizzaners, are bred at
the Kladruby Stud Farm in
Czechoslovakia

Below
Coaches and fours still bring
spectators to add to the splendours
of Royal Ascot

Right
This smart pair of show hackneys, driven by Mrs. C. Haydon, have a wonderful action

Below
Despite his contretemps with a camel, Mr. S. Watney, the President of the Driving Society, still drives a tandem—to a whitechapel cart—with a Dalmatian running in the position for which its ancestors were bred

Far right
Four-wheel, single-horse sulkies, driven in a Canadian show. Harness classes are included in almost all shows in Canada and the U.S.A.

horse because of its great age. When this leader plunged his head down as the carriage was en route, the cumbrous bridle slipped off over his ears – leaving him in an embarrassing, but happily only potentially dangerous, state of undress.

The modern coach horse must of necessity be traffic proof. It is an experience to drive on a busy road behind four horses, with motor coaches, lorries, cars and motor-bikes converging from front and rear, some of them too close for the comfort of anyone, let alone a horse. But in this age of rush and petrol fumes, what a joy it is to bowl along at a steady eight miles an hour behind four powerful, rhythmically swaying quarters, sometimes with the wide acres and lovely trees of Windsor Great Park spread to either hand, or with an excellent view over more mundane hedgerows, of growing crops and other people's gardens.

Most modern teams are made up of colour-matched, quality hunters or coach horses. A few coachmen drive hackneys, but these traditional roadsters, evolved from the old Norfolk Roadster with Thoroughbred cross, are mainly used today as show harness horses. And all over the world spectators at large shows thrill to these splendid, fiery creatures as they traverse the ring, their extravagant, brilliant action seeming to make them airborne.

Driving a four in hand may not come within the range of many, but for those with the means and ambition there is at least one school, at Stroud in Gloucestershire, where the coachman's art may yet be learned.

By 1968 the ten-year-old British Driving Society boasted a membership of 950, and about 5,000 people in Britain alone now drive a horse or pony at weekends. This is a phenomenon of the jet age that was sparked off by the petrol rationing of the last war.

The Driving Society holds meets and rallies all through the summer, trotting out together with an assortment of gigs and ralli carts, governess carts and phaetons, brakes and wagonettes, drawn by anything from a Welsh pony or cob, to a hackney or hunter. The main meet is at the Royal Windsor Horse Show where, by permission of the Queen, the members drive out from the show ground to enjoy the beauties

Above
King Feisal of Saudi Arabia, on a
State visit in 1967, drives with the
Queen and Prince Philip to take the
salute at a gallop past of the King's
Troop, Royal Horse Artillery, in
Hyde Park. The carriage is a
barouche, drawn by a pair of
Windsor Greys driven from the box.

Right
Mr. and Mrs. Nubar Gulbenkian,
seen here winning the double
harness section of an amateur
driving marathon with a pair of
Palominos, also use their horses to
go shopping

of the parks surrounding Windsor
Castle. Competitive harness classes
have just been renewed in some shows.
A mixture of obstacle or dressage driving, they provide equal excitement and
interest to competitors and spectators.

Driving is increasingly popular in the
U.S.A. Many American whips buy their
harness and sometimes their horses in
England, and come over to compete in
British shows. There are also numbers
of coaches and carriages, long forgotten in English outhouses but now re-
stored to their former beauty, being
driven around the arenas of the New
World shows.

One of the most attractive but difficult
outfits to drive is a tandem. Today's
President of the Coaching Club and
British Driving Society is an artist at the
game, but even he has his moments.

Many years ago he was driving a tandem in Beirut, negotiating the chattering crowds and street stalls, the laden, bridleless donkeys, the carts and cars and general conglomeration, with his usual expertise. But a camel proved his undoing. Our driver failed to judge the opening between the grumbling beast and an on-coming tram, the leader stuck fast, and down came both horses and the camel in a nerve-racking, kicking tangle.

Luckily no one was hurt and our driver succeeded in unravelling the mess. But it was a moment requiring his full attention, and while he placated the drivers of the camel and the tram and from a distance soothed the slobbering camel, the occupants of the tram descended unobtrusively and stole the horses' harness!

Acknowledgments

Alpha Photo Associates 82-83; American Quarter Horse Association 86; Godfrey Argent 14, 16, 17, 18-19, 20 B, 21, 25 T, 34-35, 36, 37 B, 48, 51 T, 51 CL, 52-53, 54 TL, 54 TR, 54 B-55 and endpapers, 57 T, 57 B, 58-59, 60, 61 T, 61 B, 72, 78 B, 81 B, 101, 104, 120 T, 120 C, 129 T, back jacket, back flap; Godfrey Argent, Camera Press 22; Associated Press 109 B, 123 B; Australian News & Information Bureau 44 B, 45, 47 B, 76-77, 106-107, 109 T; Austrian State Tourist Department 117 B; Author's Collection 20 T, 37 T, 37 C, 47 T, 56, 70 T, 70 B, 71, 73 L, 73 R, 82 T; J. Ayliff 51 CR, 121; Barnaby's Picture Library 6, 28-29, 75, 111, 137; Calgary Stampede Board 88 and front flap, 90, 94-95; Camera Press 23 B, 32-33, 41, 62-63, 64 T, 76 B, 92, 93, 98-99, 108, 118 T; Central Press Photos 26-27, 30, 31 B, 38-39, 50 T, 50 B, 118 B, 119, 122, 135, 138; Country Life, Sydney 84 T; Forestry Commission 68-69; Fox Photos 105 B; F.P.G. 124-125; High Commissioner for New Zealand 46; Hungarian News & Information Service 81 T; Kent Messenger 105 T; Keystone Press Agency front jacket, 89, 103 C; Kladruby Stud Farm, Czechoslovakia 134; Leslie Lane 132; Lutterworth Press 10-11; Charles Machatschek 116; J. McKeown 74; Mansell Collection 102, 133 T; Frank H. Meads 40 B; Metropolitan Museum of Art, Hewitt Fund, 1911 100; Jane J. Miller 65, 78 T, 129 B; Monty 130-131, 136 T; D. J. Murphy (Publishers) Ltd 43 TL; National Film Board of Canada 110 T; John Nestle 136 B; S. H. Nielsen 31 T; T. Parker 79; Pictorial Press 49 T, 49 B, 85, 87, 96, 110 B, 117 T; Popperfoto 80 T; Press Association 64 B, 103 B; Publifoto 114 B; Queensland Country Life 84 B, 91 B; Queensland Government Tourist Bureau 91 T; Radio Times Hulton Picture Library 76 T, 80 B, 103 T; Reed Photography 24; Rex Features 82 B; Royal Danish Ministry for Foreign Affairs 23 T; Royal Mews, Copenhagen 25 B; Barnet Saidman 114 T; D. R. Shadwell 40 T; Sport & General Press Agency 15, 43 TR, 44 T, 66 T, 115, 133 B, 139; Swedish Tourist Traffic Association 12; Syndication International 66 B; John Tarlton 126 T, 126-127, 128; The Times 42-43 B; U.P.I. 13, 112-113, 120 B, 123 T; Weekend Telegraph 97.